EVERYTHING YOU NEED TO
KNOW ABOUT ADOPTION

MAGGIE JONES is a freelance journalist. In 1975 she graduated from Exeter University with a BSc in Biological Sciences. She then worked for five years at the Family Planning Association in their Press and Publications Department, where she wrote reports and edited the quarterly journal *Family Planning Today*. She is the author of *Trying to have a Baby?* (Sheldon Press) and has also written articles which have appeared in such newspapers and magazines as the *Guardian*, *World Health* and the *Sunday Times*. She has edited a series of practical guides for the National Council for Voluntary Organizations. She is married and lives in London.

Overcoming Common Problems Series

The ABC of Eating
Coping with anorexia, bulimia and
compulsive eating
JOY MELVILLE

Acne
How it's caused and how to cure it
PAUL VAN RIEL

An A–Z of Alternative Medicine
BRENT Q. HAFEN AND KATHRYN J.
FRANDSEN

Arthritis
Is your suffering really necessary?
DR WILLIAM FOX

Birth Over Thirty
SHEILA KITZINGER

Body Language
How to read others' thoughts by their gestures
ALLAN PEASE

Calm Down
How to cope with frustration and anger
DR PAUL HAUCK

Common Childhood Illnesses
DR PATRICIA GILBERT

Coping with Depression and Elation
DR PATRICK McKEON

Curing Arthritis Cookbook
MARGARET HILLS

Curing Arthritis – The Drug-free Way
MARGARET HILLS

Depression
DR PAUL HAUCK

Divorce and Separation
ANGELA WILLANS

Enjoying Motherhood
DR BRUCE PITT

The Epilepsy Handbook
SHELAGH McGOVERN

**Everything You Need to Know about Contact
Lenses**
DR ROBERT YOUNGSON

**Everything You Need to Know about Your
Eyes**
DR ROBERT YOUNGSON

Everything You Need to Know about Shingles
DR ROBERT YOUNGSON

Family First Aid and Emergency Handbook
DR ANDREW STANWAY

Fears and Phobias
What they are and how to overcome them
DR TONY WHITEHEAD

Feverfew
A traditional herbal remedy for migraine and
arthritis
DR STEWART JOHNSON

Fight Your Phobia and Win
DAVID LEWIS

Fit Kit
DAVID LEWIS

Flying Without Fear
TESSA DUCKWORTH AND DAVID
MILLER

Goodbye Backache
DR DAVID IMRIE WITH COLLEEN
DIMSON

Guilt
Why it happens and how to overcome it
DR VERNON COLEMAN

How to Bring Up your Child Successfully
DR PAUL HAUCK

How to Control your Drinking
DRS W. MILLER AND R. MUNOZ

How to Cope with Stress
DR PETER TYRER

Overcoming Common Problems Series

Overcoming Common Problems Series

Overcoming Common Problems

EVERYTHING YOU NEED TO KNOW ABOUT ADOPTION

Maggie Jones

SHELDON PRESS
LONDON

First published in Great Britain in 1987 by
Sheldon Press, SPCK, Marylebone Road, London NW1 4DU

Thanks are due to British Agencies for Adoption and Fostering,
11, Southwark Street, London SE1 1RQ,
for permission to quote extracts from *Against the Odds*
by Catherine Macaskill © 1985,
and to Open Books Publishing Limited for an extract from
Adoption: a Second Chance by Barbara Tizard.

British Library Cataloguing in Publication Data
Jones, Maggie
  Everything you need to know about adoption.
  — (Overcoming common problems)
  1. Adoption — Great Britain
  I. Title   II. Series
  362.7'34'0941   HV875.7.G7

  ISBN 0-85969-545-X
  ISBN 0-85969-546-8 Pbk

Filmset by Deltatype, Ellesmere Port, Cheshire
Printed in Great Britain by
Richard Clay Ltd, Bungay, Suffolk

Contents

Introduction

What is adoption?

Adopting a child means bringing him or her into your life and your heart and giving the care that you would give to your own blood children. Adoption is forever, in the same sense that the children you give birth to are forever; you bear the legal responsibilities for them, you take the consequences of their actions, you provide the shelter and support through their developing years, and you help them out into independence when it is time. In return, you will share in the joys and sorrows of parenthood and experience a deep relationship that would otherwise have been denied you.

Adoption is not about possession. Adoptive parents do not possess their children any more than natural parents do. But it has been shown repeatedly by research, and is the experience of all people who work with or have a wide experience of young children, that a child wants and needs a family to which he or she feels he belongs for always, or at least till he is ready to leave. All the evidence shows that this is best for the child. In the words of one adoption worker, 'Adoption is no longer a secret, private way for childless parents to procure a child and pass it off as their "own". It is a public way of caring for a child in the best possible way, that is within a stable, caring family.'

How adoption has changed

The adoption scene has changed out of all recognition over the past fifteen to twenty years. Anyone who is considering adopting a child needs to be aware of what these changes are and why they have occurred. In 1968 there were 25,000 adoptions in England and Wales; three-quarters of these were adoptions by strangers to the child, rather than by step-parents. By 1984, there were fewer than 8,000 adoptions; over half of these were adoptions by step-parents, and of the remaining, less than 1,000 were healthy white babies under the age of one.

The change has come about because of a dramatic fall in the numbers of unwanted pregnancies and births. This is because of better family planning services and the availability of modern methods of contraception; because of the passing of the 1967 Abortion Act which enabled many women with unwanted pregnancies to have the pregnancy terminated safely rather than risking the back streets; and because of the increased acceptance that unmarried mothers should keep and bring up their babies on their own or with family and friends if they choose to.

The shortage of healthy white babies for adoption brought about a sudden revolution in adoption practice. Over a period of about five years the idea of adoption as a service for childless couples gave way to the concept of adoption as a service for children needing families. Research which was carried out in the early 1970s in the famous *Children Who Wait* study showed that if a pre-school or primary-school-aged child had been in care for as long as six months, the chances of returning to their family were slim. Most of these children had no contact at all with their families and would still be in care at the age of eighteen.

The majority of these children in care had not until then been considered suitable for adoption. They were 'children with special needs' – emotionally damaged by experiences in their early lives and by the effects of living in an institution. This had given them behaviour problems and created difficulties in their abilities to make and keep relationships with others. Most were boys, and about a quarter were black or of mixed parentage. More than half also had brothers or sisters in care, and since these were all the family they had, no one wished to separate them. They also included children who were mentally and physically handicapped children whose parents had rejected them at birth.

Once adoption agencies and the public became aware of these 'children who wait', the idea that suitable parents *could* be found for the children began to grow. Experiences in America showed that with a more aggressive approach to finding families for children with special needs, children previously considered as 'unplaceable' could be found families. Infertile couples who realised they were unlikely to be offered the 'healthy white baby' of their dreams started to consider adopting older children, black or mixed-race children, or handicapped babies.

Many of the families who came forward already had children of their own and wanted to add to their families and use their parenting skills to help these special and needy children. Many were parents who would have been considered completely inappropriate to adopt the healthy babies for whom there was so much competition. Age, class, housing conditions, whether the mother worked or not, whether they were single or married, all seemed less relevant than whether they could meet the special needs of the child.

At the moment it is estimated that there may be as many as 20,000 children in the care of local authorities or in hospitals in Britain who could be placed with families for adoption. So while there is a shortage of healthy babies there is no shortage of children to adopt.

Recent changes in the law on adoption in Britain under the Children Act 1975 which has gradually come into force, have also had their impact in changing the nature of adoption today. It is now possible for all adopted people to have access to their original birth records with the names of their mother or both parents, place of birth and so on, once they reach the age of eighteen. This may enable the adopted child to trace and make contact with his or her birth parents. Some prospective adopters may be discouraged by this new law, as they may fear the natural parents being traced later on, but for adopted people, information about their origins is of vital importance. It also makes it more difficult for adoptive parents to conceal this from their children, but adoption agencies now advocate complete honesty and openness about the fact of adoption from the outset.

Secondly, private adoptions were made illegal in 1982 unless the child's mother places the child for adoption with a close relative. This now makes it impossible for someone legally to adopt a baby they know of through a friend, clergyman, doctor or relative, or to make special arrangements through an abortion agency when a mother is refused an abortion because her pregnancy is too far advanced. All adoptions must now go through a recognized adoption agency – this is to ensure that the child's needs are best met by adoption, that the prospective parents are right for that particular child and that the legal requirements have been met. An adoption agency can be either a local authority or an approved adoption society.

The change in the law also rules out the possibility of someone choosing to continue with an unwanted pregnancy because she knows a childless couple who would like to adopt. She would not be able to guarantee that this couple would be chosen by an adoption agency as the best for that child. With the shortage of healthy babies for adoption, there was evidence that money was sometimes changing hands in such arrangements and that the child's interests were not the priority.

Other changes have made the position easier for those children whose parents have demonstrated a consistent inability to care for the child but have held out against adoption. Until recently a parent could leave a child in care indefinitely and by refusing to allow anyone to adopt, jeopardize the child's chance of a stable family life. The Children Act 1975 states quite clearly that agencies and courts must 'give first consideration to the need to safeguard and promote (the child's) welfare throughout his childhood'. This has increasingly meant that agencies have gone ahead and placed a child for adoption despite the fact that the parents have refused to consent to the adoption. If the mother has changed her mind several times, or the child has been in care for a long time and/or the mother or father have shown that they really cannot care for the child, and have abandoned, neglected or ill-treated him, the court may grant an adoption order anyway. However, the wishes of the parents, both natural and adoptive, are given greater weight in adoption proceedings than they are in most other legal proceedings related to children.

These provisions have caused considerable opposition and concern in some quarters. Parents whose children have gone into care through no fault of their own, because their circumstances are exceptionally difficult – poor housing, a marriage or relationship splitting up, family illness or death, financial crisis – now live in fear that their children may be taken away from them for good. People argue, quite rightly, that the child of well-off parents may be equally neglected or ill-treated – working mothers who leave children all day with a succession of uncaring nannies, child-minders or babysitters are one example, or children caught in the crossfire of divorcing parents – but because the children are well dressed, the home well cared for and the parents can put on a good front to teachers, social workers and the police, these children are almost never taken into care. The risk of losing their children is another cross which poor families have to bear.

Indeed, adoption is very much mistrusted by some people because it is seen as taking the children of the poor and giving them to the rich. The people whose children go into care and may be placed for adoption are among the most powerless in our society. The reasons why their children go into care may be more to do with inadequate housing or homelessness, the fact that mothers have to work to make ends meet and cannot afford proper childminding, or that they are relatively new to this country and have no network of relatives or friends who can step in and take the children in a family crisis, than with any maltreatment or severe neglect.

Some parents who in the end gave up their children for adoption or who continue to visit them while in care in institutions or foster homes did not want to give them up and would have kept them if only there had been some financial help from government, perhaps in the form of more realistic child allowances, suitable day-care nurseries so that mothers could go out to work, suitable support services to help them deal with crises in the family such as divorce, illness or the birth of a new baby, and better accommodation. There is no doubt that while these conditions do not exist families will still be split up against their will and it will be the children who suffer most.

It is ironic that the class element in adoption is now being turned upside down. In the past, middle-class couples tended to adopt working-class children. This still goes on, of course, but now it is often working-class couples who adopt severely handicapped or emotionally disturbed children who have been rejected by their middle-class families.

Many of the old myths and fears about adoption have also been turned on their head by the experiences of recent years. It used to be felt that adopting children was second best to having your own blood children, and that if you did adopt, you should adopt a child as close as possible in appearance to yourself so 'people would never know'. People were afraid that 'bad blood' would show and that the child of a criminal would be more likely to turn out a criminal. People feared that they would fail to understand their children because they did not share the same family traits or understand the child's personality. Indeed, sometimes parents who feared these things put the kinds of pressures on the child which led to the very problems which they feared.

Research has now shown that most of these fears are unfounded. One study of 150 children born to 75 mentally retarded women showed that only ten per cent were mentally handicapped. Another study showed that children whose fathers had been criminals were no more likely to become criminals than other children if brought up in a stable family. Of course, children do inherit their personalities, their potential intelligence and their appearance from their parents, but a look at ordinary families will show how much those characteristics can vary between brothers and sisters. Far more important in developing a healthy and able personality are a secure family and home, and loving parents. Besides, intelligence itself is not as important as what a person does with the abilities he or she has. And as for looks, many adopted people or step-children find people chorus 'Don't you look like your mother' when there is no blood link. People see what they want and expect to see, and mannerisms copied from the ones we love and live with can be more important in people's appearance than looks alone.

Many people feel that the blood bond is the most significant factor in determining whether they love a child. This lies behind the view that children are better off with their natural parents as well as the view that you cannot love another person's child as much as your own. There is no evidence that this is true. One study of a group of children who had been in care since early babyhood and who were then either adopted or returned to their natural mothers, showed that a greater proportion of adoptive parents felt love for their child and felt this was returned than did the natural families. The natural families seemed more pre-occupied with having 'missed out' on their children's babyhood and many of them had other younger children demanding care and attention who took precedence over them. Many natural parents in fact do not want their children in the first place, but conceive them accidentally and feel pressurized by society into giving birth to them and keeping them, while all adoptive parents have shown that they really do want a child, and have gone to considerable lengths to find one.

The lack of a blood tie in adoptive families is also behind such fears as 'you will never really understand the child' or 'they will turn against you when they are older'. Again, there is absolutely no evidence for these fears, and in fact children are far less likely to 'turn against' adoptive parents who have cared for them than against natural ones who have not. Love is not a matter of an abstract emotion. It is to do with spending time, giving attention and care to a child and meeting his needs, slowly building a bond that is far stronger than blood.

Becoming parents

In any happy family, the parents want to provide a stable base for their children, to let them develop and grow to become their own people, and then become independent, move away, form stable relationships and have families of their own. Ideas of possession, of wanting the children to be what you would like them to be, to do the jobs you would have liked them to do or would have liked to do yourselves, create conflict and unhappiness in any family.

The best adoptive parents are those who would also make the best natural parents. They are happy to provide a stable home and not expect the world. They have a strong enough sense of their own needs to know where to draw the line and lay down house rules, and they are not upset if 'their' children don't turn out quite as expected. Because they don't have strong feelings

7

that 'their' children should be like themselves, they are more tolerant of different personalities within the family. If they have a good relationship themselves, they will know not to let a child try to invade or weaken that relationship, and that will help them enormously when a child, particularly one with an insecure background, tests out his parents.

Thinking about adoption is not an easy matter. Many would-be parents rush into ideas of adoption as the natural next step when they are told they are infertile. However, such people may have had little time to get over the grief and distress of not being able to have children of their own, and have not been able to think clearly about what adoption might really mean to them. Similarly, people who decide to adopt after a child has died should allow plenty of time to get over their loss, to be sure that they want a child for his or her own sake and not just to replace the one who has been lost.

Couples who already have children may want to adopt for a number of reasons.

We had two children, a girl and a boy, then aged nine and six. We both wanted a big family but felt that today, with the planet overpopulated and with so many children in need of love and homes, it seemed wrong to go on bringing more children into the world. Our children were both healthy and happy and we felt we were good as parents, and we also had a big house and enough money. It seemed just the right thing to adopt another two children who no one else wanted, even if they had special problems or handicaps.

I loved having children but when we had our third, Dawn, I was shattered to be told soon after the birth that she had Down's Syndrome. But we found that when we accepted her and gave her love and attention she blossomed and, contrary to everything we were told to expect, she crawled at eighteen months, walked at two and a half and at six is toilet-trained and going to a special school. When she went there and the house was quiet again the idea came to me: why not adopt an abandoned Down's Syndrome baby and give him or her the loving start we have been able to give our own little girl?

It's very important that you think about what you want to get out of adopting a child before you begin. Asking yourself some basic questions can help put things in perspective. How well can you cope with rudeness, disagreeable or disturbed behaviour? Are you firm enough to help a child into a routine and to stop unacceptable behaviour while still being kind to him? Do you love babies but not get on well with teenagers, or is it the other way round? Above all, what particular handicaps can you cope with – a family which sets high store on academic achievement might be unable to cope with a mentally handicapped child but find helping a child with severe physical disabilities to learn and prosper very fulfilling. What particular qualities do you think that you can give a child?

Adoption agencies will help you think all these things through before considering an individual child. One would-be adoptive mother who with her husband was accepted by an agency describes the process like this:

The agency were very thorough in getting us to think about the kind of child we would accept. We had a five-year-old boy born to us, and very much wanted a second child to complete the family, and didn't want James to be an only child, but I didn't get pregnant again. Because of our age (I was 35) it was clear that we couldn't adopt a newborn baby, and this agency had a rule that the child you adopted had to be the youngest in the family, which meant a child of four or less. This meant that we were really being asked to consider a child with a handicap or behavioural problems.

We had many interviews and group meetings, which showed us how we had to take into account the kind of people we were, our strengths and weaknesses, and we also had to take James's needs into account. We decided that it wouldn't be right for us to adopt a severely mentally handicapped child – we took a lot of pride in James's abilities and wouldn't have had the patience with a very slow child. I feel that having a child is very much tied up with promise for the future and with a severely handicapped child I wouldn't have been able to feel that. We would have been prepared, however, to cope with an emotionally damaged small child and to have helped in the process of healing – there would have been some promise there.

Adoption today is both more difficult and more rewarding than it used to be. More difficult in that there are few healthy babies to adopt, but more rewarding in that the challenges are so much greater. Parents are being asked to think about issues and give of themselves in a way they have never been asked before. Even if you think you would never be able to adopt a handicapped or emotionally disturbed child, read on; many people who thought so once are now the proud parents of a child or children they would never have dreamed of.

1

How to Go About It

If you want to adopt, the first step is to apply to one of the two hundred adoption agencies in England, Wales and Scotland and ask to go on their waiting list. This is not as simple as it sounds. The majority of these adoption agencies are part of local authority departments, but some are voluntary agencies like Dr Barnardo's, the Church of England Children's Society and the Catholic Children's Society. Although some of these agencies are national and have regional offices throughout the country, not every area will be covered. People living in one area might have a large choice of agencies and others very few. Some agencies may have large numbers of children available for adoption, others none at all. Some agencies consider requests from parents at a great distance but most concentrate on people living within their own boundaries. Most agencies will look further afield on behalf of children with special needs.

The British Agencies for Adoption and Fostering (BAAF) produce a booklet called *Adopting a Child* which provides a list of adoption agencies and maps showing where they are located. The booklet also tells you whether each agency limits their work to people of a particular religion, whether they have age limits and other rules they might apply. It also explains what adoption involves and how to go about it. You then need to contact an agency directly to find out if there are any children available to adopt at the time you're applying – some people apply to more than one, and the responses vary. Because there are so many applicants, especially for babies, many agencies have to close their books from time to time and may be unable to say when they are likely to open them again. If you are looking for a child with special needs, the process should be easier.

For parents applying to adopt babies or small children, many agencies set upper age limits which are likely to be around 35 or 40. This may simply be done to help limit the numbers of people wanting to adopt young children but agencies also say they are concerned about large age gaps between parents and children, and whether they will have the energy to cope with broken nights with a young baby and a difficult teenager when they are in their 50s or more, and that older parents are more likely to suffer illness or die, thus further depriving a child who has already lost one set of parents. However, many natural parents have children later and often make better parents. One couple turned down for adoption on grounds of age expressed considerable contempt for the agency's motives:

> They gave all sorts of reasons, like wouldn't you be the odd ones out when you met the child from school, and how would the child feel about having old parents. But when we said we were prepared to adopt a black child (this was a few years ago now) or a child with some handicap their attitude changed. This really annoyed me, and I asked 'Does that mean it doesn't matter if a black child or handicapped child has old parents? Won't they be just as ashamed of having us meet them at school as any other child? In fact, isn't it even more important for them to have "ordinary" parents?' It was a question they just couldn't answer, in fact I think it embarrassed them.

Most agencies specify that couples must be married and for some agencies, for example Catholic agencies, a past divorce is not acceptable. Others may set rules on race, for example that black or mixed-race children must be placed with black parents (see section on transracial adoption).

Some adoption agencies have a very formal approach and prefer to be contacted by letter, in which case you should write giving details of your ages, occupations, religion, length of marriage, if either of you have any children and their ages, and any other relevant details. You should mention if you have applied to other agencies as well and also say if you've fostered a child or have any other experience of working with or looking after children. You should also give as much information as possible about the kind of child you would like to adopt. Fix your horizons as widely as possible, although of course you shouldn't mislead an agency by saying you would adopt an older child if you really want a baby or toddler or that you want a handicapped child if you are just thinking of some minor physical handicap.

Some agencies suggest that you attend information meetings which the agency holds regularly, where a number of interested couples are gathered together and the agency gives details of how they work and the kind of children they have available for adoption. These can be a very useful way of talking to other couples wanting to adopt, and meeting the adoption agency workers on a less formal basis. Do take up a suggestion to attend: you can learn a lot from these meetings. They are not just aimed at putting you off as this person thought:

> I decided to see what happened, so finally I picked up the phone and rang one agency which didn't seem to have too many restrictions. The woman who answered the phone said, 'Can I help you?' and I said, 'Yes, I'm interested in adopting.' Then she said, straight away before I could go any further, rather rudely, 'You realise that there aren't any white babies for adoption.' And I said, 'Yes, I do know that, we're not particularly interested in a white baby.' So then she said, 'Well, we prefer black babies to go to black parents, you know,' and I said, 'Oh.' There was a pause, and then she asked some questions, such as how old was I, how old was my husband. When I said I was 30 and he was 45, there was another long pause, and then she said, 'Would you be prepared to adopt an older or handicapped child?' And I said, 'Yes, I think we might, we'd like to look into it.' So then she suggested we wrote in and went to one of their regular information meetings, where they get a number of interested couples together and give them more information. I put the phone down and burst into tears, she seemed so rude and unconcerned with what I might be feeling. But then I suppose they get dozens of calls like that every day.

Usually the approach will be somewhat different if you want to adopt a child who is considerably handicapped or comes from a very disturbed background, having experienced violence, a history of disruption of previous foster placements or a long period in an institution. Some children have known many homes by the time they reach their teens or sometimes earlier. Adoption agencies are now waiving all restrictions on adopters for such children, so that older couples, single people, working mothers, the unemployed and handicapped people are all considered as potential parents if they feel they can offer something to a particular child. These people are frequently not the kind of people who would decide to adopt in the way that childless couples do, so adoption agencies have had to find new ways of attracting them. The advertising of children through the press, radio and television and through special adoption catalogues has been very successful in finding parents for hard-to-place children.

One example is BAAF's 'Be My Parent' scheme. It consists of a large loose-leafed book, updated monthly, which features photographs of children waiting for new families who are in the care of different agencies around the country. The text gives brief personal details, why the child needs to be adopted, and the kind of family or parent the child is seeking. Often the children themselves – if they are old enough – are involved in writing the 'advertisements'. Since the scheme started in 1980 it has placed over three hundred children for adoption. If you are interested in seeing the book, ask at your local adoption agency, or telephone the Be My Parent office in London to see where your nearest book is held. You should also keep a look out for the advertisements which appear regularly in newspapers.

People who have responded to advertisements in the press or through the 'Be My Parent' scheme usually refer to the extraordinary feeling of recognition that they have when they see the picture of the child they go on to adopt. While the idea in theory of adopting a multiply-handicapped child may seem impossible or unthinkable, someone may simply see and fall for a particular child and, because they are seeing the child and not the handicap, find themselves able to accept any degree of disability. It is usually a highly individual response, sometimes rather like falling in love. Those running the scheme say that some people come forward convinced that there must be a queue of people wanting that particular child and are such that they must be too late. They may be the only people to have shown any interest in that child whatsoever.

Adoption parties

Another approach used by agencies is the 'adoption party'. Many children have had so many disappointments that being introduced to a chain of prospective parents who want to go no further becomes an increasingly harrowing experience. Similarly, many would-be parents find themselves pressurised in such a situation because they cannot bear to say 'no' and disappoint the child. Often the atmosphere at such introductions is tense and uneasy. The idea behind an adoption party is that it is much more casual, doesn't give the prospective adopters and children such high expectations and can be seen as simply an enjoyable event for all.

A number of prospective adopters and children needing families are invited to a party or some other kind of social event where there will be food, children's games and so on. Some of the parents may have particular children in mind or the adoption agency workers have a child in mind for them, others may simply be interested to see what happens. If a child or children and would-be parents hit it off, this can be pursued later. Often adoption parties have extraordinary consequences. One couple approached an agency wanting to adopt a handicapped baby boy and were invited to an adoption party. There they fell in love with a family of three noisy girls with a deprived background who wanted nothing more than to go away to live with them then and there. A very successful adoption was subsequently arranged.

The next hurdle

Even if you have seen the child you want through such a scheme, you still need to be interviewed by the agency and accepted as suitable adopters like any other couple. This is the next hurdle of the adoption process. There will normally be lengthy and intensive interviews with the social worker dealing with your application. The social worker will want to get to know you well, meet you in your home, and ask all kinds of searching questions about your attitude to parenthood, your marriage,

15

even your sex life. At first this may seem an unnecessary intrusion, but the social worker will want to make sure that your marriage is happy and stable, that you really do want children and that you would make 'good enough' parents. He or she will also be wanting to match a child with you as individuals and to do this will need to know you quite well.

Some of the questions may seem hard to answer. Why do you want children? What do you think that you can give to a child? are two common ones. As one prospective adopter said, 'Why does *anyone* want children? Nobody asks natural parents such questions'. Because the social worker wants to know the truth, the questions may seem complex. 'Do you have a happy marriage?' will simply get the answer 'Yes', whether it's true or not. A question like 'What do you think is the best thing about your marriage? And the worst?' is much more likely to elicit the truth and give someone insight into the situation.

Similarly, you may be asked questions about your own childhood, how your parents brought you up, and where you feel they succeeded and failed. 'I remember many of the searching questions she asked us, such as "Is there anything you would do in bringing up a child which would be different from the way you were brought up?" ' It can be difficult to answer such questions, but it is best to be natural and answer as fully and openly as you can. Nobody is looking for perfection, they just want to make sure that you are not covering up something in your childhood which could make it hard for you to care for a child. Sometimes something that seems to be a problem can turn into a strength:

I was afraid to say that my father was an alcoholic and that I hardly ever saw him after the age of six. But in the end I came out with it and the social worker was sympathetic. She asked what I felt about it now and whether it had influenced my own marriage. I said that it had made me wait till I was absolutely sure that this was the right man to marry and that it had made me aware of how important stability and a caring father were to a child. I didn't get the feeling that this revelation had done damage to our chances in any way, in fact it gave us an opportunity to really explain how committed we were to our

16

marriage and to caring for children, giving them the loving family I didn't have.

Many couples interested in adopting say they feel they are being considered as having ulterior motives for wanting to adopt a child. Don't worry about this; be as open and natural as possible.

You will also often be asked to have a medical to make sure that you are both healthy and, for some agencies, if you are wanting to adopt a baby, you may need proof that you are infertile.

Once the social worker has finished the assessment the decision will come before an adoption panel, for you to be approved or not approved by that agency. If you are not approved, this can seem a crushing disappointment, but this does not necessarily mean that you won't be accepted elsewhere:

We had applied to adopt at a social services department. We were rather inexperienced and, although we didn't like or get on with the social worker, we went on with a series of five or six interviews where we seemed to repeat everything we had said on every previous occasion, without ever getting on to discuss what we felt was really important. After the assessment we had to wait over three months before we were turned down. We asked to know the reasons, and when they were given they sounded absurd: that our income was too low; that I was too young (at 22); that since we could have children of our own they felt it would be unwise to adopt. They just hadn't seemed to grasp that we wanted to adopt a handicapped child who no one else wanted.

We heard about an agency that placed severely handicapped children in our area and applied to them. The treatment we had was completely different. We were welcomed, the discussions were long and discussed every aspect of adopting a handicapped child, we were taken to visit a foster home and asked to go to information meetings and an adoption party. It took some time to find us the right child, but we never felt afraid to say 'I'm sorry, this one's not for us' or felt that this affected our chances. They told us there's the right child for every family and, in the end, we found him.

Applying to adoption agencies takes time and patience and it's important not to be put off, even if your first contacts seem disappointing. After all, there is a very long process to go through before a child can become legally yours and you will need a great deal of energy and commitment to see it through.

Adopting from abroad

When a couple are unable to adopt a healthy baby in their own country, it is natural to wonder whether they couldn't adopt one of the millions of children abandoned at birth or living in institutions in the world's poor countries. Scenes of the plight of babies and young children in areas of drought, famine, war or dreadful poverty are brought vividly to attention on television and with every appeal for financial help from agencies like Oxfam and Save the Children come hundreds of offers to adopt a child.

The problem is that though a large number of these children will not live, the majority of them are not unwanted. They are desperately wanted by their parents who long to give them health and life, they are wanted by their communities who need young people to build a better life and they are wanted by their countries who see their children as their main resource for development in the future.

Many people who work for Third World aid agencies or hold places in governments in the Third World are highly critical of people who want to adopt such children. They argue that if people in Western countries can afford to spend thousands of pounds on adopting a child, could they not spend that money to enable the child to grow up within his or her own family, culture and country rather than being taken abroad to ease the heartache of an infertile couple? Many agencies run 'foster a child' schemes whereby you give money regularly to pay for the food, clothing, schooling and medical treatment of a child in the Third World and receive information about that child's progress and often correspond with him and his family – agencies argue that this is really a better way to help a child.

There is also a political element in opposition to adoption from abroad. Many Third World countries are recovering their sense of cultural identity and pride after years of colonial occupation, and see this export of their children as a further aspect of colonialism. They feel that Western couples take their children in the same spirit as they took the countries' natural resources, grew crops geared to Western markets and removed art treasures to Western museums. Widely publicised cases where babies have been stolen or mothers have been paid large sums to part with them by unscrupulous middlemen to sell to Western couples have made people increasingly suspicious of intercountry adoption. Even more worrying is the fact that people in war-torn or famine-stricken countries may put their children up for adoption simply to procure their protection, and then wish they could have them back when the situation has improved.

Further, the concept of legal adoption with its breaking of all legal ties between the child and his blood relatives is completely unknown in many cultures. Islamic law does not recognize it at all. In cultures where people live in tribal groups and extended families a child cannot be parentless as the wider family will consider him as theirs. Children often move from one member of the family's care to another, for example for schooling or to help with work, and the idea of permanent adoption can be misunderstood. Few African or Asian countries see legal, Western-style adoption by strangers as a solution for orphaned or abandoned children.

When the numbers of healthy babies available for adoption fell throughout Europe in the 1970s, almost every country other than Britain looked abroad as an alternative. In Sweden some 1500 children a year are adopted from overseas and there are several government approved agencies which find children on a couple's behalf. This pattern is repeated across Europe. Although in many cases the adoptions are arranged privately by couples themselves or through unregulated organizations, intercountry adoption did not happen on a large scale in Britain for two main reasons. Firstly, local authorities were the largest single group of adoption agencies and they had to look first to their responsibilities in finding homes for the children in their care, rather than acting as an agency to find couples a healthy baby. The voluntary agencies responded to the same priorities, seeing adoption first as a service for children needing families. Secondly, British governments were increasingly concerned about what they saw as high levels of immigration into Britain by British-passport-holding residents of Asian, West Indian and African former colonies. Attempts were being made to tighten up immigration laws, which might look rather silly if large numbers of white British couples were freely bringing foreign babies into the country.

So what happens if a British couple do decide to adopt from the Third World? The answer is that it can be done, but because there are no official channels the process is lengthy, complex, expensive, often heart-rending, and a couple has to do it all more-or-less unsupported.

First, you have to pick your country. Many Third World nations have passed legislation making it very hard for foreigners to adopt – Indonesia, for example, has ruled that a foreign couple must be resident there for at least seven years before they can apply to adopt. In other countries, legislation may vary from state to state and, to complicate matters further, although the law may allow foreign parents to adopt, the judges responsible for granting adoption orders in any district have a great deal of discretion. If a judge does not personally agree with intercountry adoption, he may find reasons for not allowing it to go through. It is important to check all these things in advance before starting your quest.

One couple's experience

Parent to Parent Information on Adoption Services (PPIAS) may be able to help by putting you in touch with other couples who have adopted successfully and pass on useful contacts. However, the situation is changing all the time and there are many dangers, as illustrated by this couple's experience.

We were given the address of a lawyer in Bolivia who we wrote to along with some other contacts. He wrote back and said he could arrange it, and to contact a woman in England who had adopted a baby through him, who would act as an intermediary. He told us we would probably have to go to Bolivia in June or July to pick up our baby. We contacted the woman and I suppose our suspicions should have been aroused, as she acted in a very guarded and suspicious way. She told us what papers we should take and who should authenticate them when we arrived, but then astonished us by later ringing us and saying we should go next week in the place of an Israeli couple who for some reason were not going to go ahead. We had to send a wire to the lawyer in Bolivia with our names and a name to give the baby, who had presumably already been found for the other couple. We had to send $300 to this woman at once – she said her husband had already sent it on our behalf and we must pay them back. Also we had to go to Brazil to pick up the baby. It all sounded odd, and she refused to answer any of our questions. We flew to São Paulo with her, and on the journey she again refused to answer our queries and simply said that 'she knew how to bribe the immigration officials' and so on. All she would say was that we were going to meet another English couple there, we would see the papers and the babies and be able to take them home.

When we arrived at the hotel we met the other couple and were given the papers to look at. When we saw them our hearts sank, because they were clearly forged. They were poor photocopies with our names and other details filled in over the top of something else. We didn't see how they would fool any officials and we didn't know who the baby belonged to, whether the parents had really agreed to the adoption or not, whether the baby was healthy (there was no medical report), how they had got from Bolivia to Brazil, and there was no way to check anything. We had to make up our minds on the spot, and we decided we couldn't go ahead. It was clearly illegal, and worse than that, we couldn't live with not knowing if the baby had been stolen, what his background was, and so on. It all seemed incredibly sordid and shabby. So we excused ourselves and, of course, in a terribly distressed state, we went back home. It taught us that you have to be there on the spot to find your own baby and be convinced that the circumstances are right and everything is above board and that the parents genuinely want the child to be adopted, before going ahead with such a step.

Once you have decided where to go to look for your baby, it is best to follow the official procedure for adopting a child from abroad. Anyone considering this should approach the Home Office at an early stage for details of procedures and requirements. It is estimated that about fifty babies a year enter the country this way, as well as a number of others through the 'back door'. Procedures will vary from country to country but probably, first of all, you need to have a 'home study' carried out by a social worker to show that you are suitable to adopt. This can be done by a local authority if you are waiting to adopt through a local authority adoption agency, or you can have a private study done, through a voluntary adoption agency, if this is not possible – though this may be illegal under the Children Act 1975. Many local authorities will not do a home study if they know you want to adopt from abroad. A home study is time-consuming and such requests may annoy hard-pressed departments trying to meet the needs of children in their care. One mother who adopted from abroad had been approved already as a foster parent for teenagers, though her age and the fact that she was no longer married meant that she was not approved for adopting younger children. 'The Indian authorities accepted this study although it was three years out of date, and I got a private social worker to confirm that my circumstances were still acceptable.' Getting a home study is in the baby's best interests, may help you to formalize the adoption abroad, and help you to get the sympathy of officials when your adoption has to be formalized in British law.

Couples can do without this, however. Detailed character references from figures such as doctors, lawyers and priests can suffice to convince the authorities abroad that you are suitable parents. You may also need reports from doctors saying that you are in good health, giving the reasons why you are infertile, and a report of your economic situation and perhaps photographs of the home where you live and will be bringing up the child. Usually it is then necessary to go to the country where you want to adopt with all the documentation and find the baby you want, and then wait while the adoption is legalized in that country before you can take any steps to bring the baby home. The prospective adopters do not always have to be present at this stage, but usually it helps.

If you succeed in finding a baby and getting the adoption formalized in the child's own country, you then have to go to the consulate and apply for an entry visa to bring the child back into Britain. In fact this procedure can take months, during which time the baby is getting older and you have to deal with the uncertainties and make arrangements for the child's care if you are not able to wait in the country with him. An application for entry clearance for a child adopted from abroad is considered by the Home Office and the DHSS. The DHSS must be able to advise the Home Office that there is no reason why the adoption cannot be granted when an application is eventually made to a British court. In order to make this decision, they will ask the local authority to make a home study to establish that the prospective adopters are suitable, and set this alongside information from other sources about the child's situation in his country of origin. Intending adopters have to pay for the preparation of statements, translation of documents and so on. It is not surprising that many couples try to avoid this part of the procedure and simply fly home, turning up at the airport in the hope that the officials will take pity and let them through.

In theory, the immigration officials have three choices: to let the baby through, granting a temporary entry visa until such time as the adoption can come before a British court; take the child into care; or deport him. In practice, it appears that the babies are always let through. The alternatives to letting the baby go with its new parents are certainly not in the child's best interests, and it would be hard to argue a case for it unless, of course, the numbers became much greater and there is pressure to make people go through the official route.

The implications of this are, in fact, enormous. It means that, while the children and other relatives of British citizens of Asian, West Indian and African origin are frequently refused entry into the country, or have to submit to blood tests to prove their identity before they can come in, white couples can bring in unrelated children with comparative ease. The whole situation is very unsatisfactory, and there are fears that if intercountry adoption were made easier, the numbers of children coming in would grow and that the immigration authorities would be placed in a politically quite explosive situation.

Despite this, the pressure is on some adoption agencies to provide an intercountry service as well as their other adoption work. These agencies would deal only with official adoption agencies and orphanages in the countries concerned and would help ease the paperwork. This would help couples wanting to adopt, make channels clearer for the officials, and help cut out the unscrupulous middlemen who are making money out of illegal and costly transactions. There is no doubt that some couples are so desperate to adopt that they will pay large sums of money for a child whose origin is uncertain. Agencies might also be able to help place children unlikely to be found homes in their own countries, such as illegitimate children or children of mixed parentage.

After the baby has been granted entry, you will then need to apply to adopt the child in the normal way, which entails going through the British courts. Certain foreign adoptions are recognized in the UK and children adopted in these countries do not have to be re-adopted in the UK. They include most new Commonwealth countries and all UK dependent territories, most European countries and the USA. Otherwise, once the child is in the care of prospective adopters and they have applied for an adoption order, the child is considered as a foster child and will be supervised by the social services. They will want to see that the child is in good hands. Some social workers have been very hostile to people who have adopted a foreign baby, especially in local authority areas where black babies are only placed for adoption with black families (see transracial adoption). Many resent spending time on intercountry adoptions while children on their caseloads wait longer to find an adoptive family.

I was very nervous about the social worker coming to visit. The authorities were very cold and made it quite clear that they didn't approve, although two-year-old Anna was there and was so obviously happy and thriving. I knew that there wasn't anything they could do, that they couldn't take her away unless we were alcoholics or showed evidence of beating her but all the same I was frightened. I was also afraid that my husband would get angry and say something rude.

Social workers are, however, concerned at how the child will adjust to growing up in a different culture and many also want to advise parents on common post-adoption problems, how to tell the child about their past, and give guidance on dealing with racial prejudice.

So much for the theory. How intercountry adoption works out in practice is shown very well by the following couple's experience.

We had tried to adopt in this country but were finally turned down on grounds of age to adopt a baby, which was what we both wanted. We decided to adopt from abroad and made enquiries through friends and through PPIAS, who gave us addresses of people who'd been successful. We then wrote all over the world and waited to see what happened. A woman wrote from Rio to say she could help us but couldn't get any babies out now, but that she'd write in six months time, which to our surprise she did. She was doing it because she believed it was best for babies and parents and she didn't want to be paid, though she said we would need money to pay the judge. So off we went with our return tickets, which in theory we couldn't change, but which we had to do three times, as time dragged on. We were there in the end about six weeks.

We met another couple who had just adopted in the hotel and they gave us their contacts and introduced us to an interpreter who took us to a lawyer in Rio. We had to give all our papers – character and medical references, etc. – to the judge of the minors' court who would authorize us to go to the official orphanage. We went to visit there and found that no-one was very helpful. We definitely wanted a baby, while all the children we were offered were at least a year old. We found three healthy babies and asked if we could adopt them and they instantly became vague, saying they didn't know if they were really abandoned, 'we don't know if you can have them'. We went to see the judge, the social worker, various officials, but we couldn't get any clear answer. In the end we decided they were just trying to put us off. We later were told that official orphanages are given money on a head count and weren't very anxious to give children away for that reason.

The interpreter the couple we'd met put us in touch with said we'd be better off going to the hospital in the region where they had succeeded in finding their baby. So we went to all the maternity hospitals in the area (there were seven of them) and to call on social services in two towns, all in a period of three days. Everyone said no. Some places said we don't give babies to white couples, others that there were Brazilian couples waiting to adopt. Some were helpful and said that they wanted to help but there weren't any suitable babies and they'd get in touch. In the meantime we ran into other couples, mostly German, all doing the same thing. We got very depressed at this stage. Then we found a nun running a foster home who said that she knew there was a suitable baby in the first hospital we'd visited where they'd said they didn't give babies to foreign couples. So we went back and asked to see this particular baby, who was a boy and five weeks old. The mother was very ill and was in the hospital and said she wanted the baby adopted. We knew instantly when we saw him that this was the baby for us. We went straight to the lawyer we'd met in a local town who had seemed honest. (He told us, 'If you find a baby I can arrange the adoption but I can't find a baby for you'.) The parents had to be interviewed by the judge and sign papers – a hospital doctor had to check the baby and see that he was healthy – we had to wait a week while all the papers went to the judge and the adoption was granted. Once it was clear that we were going to adopt him the hospital staff became friendly and let us in to feed him. We stayed there for two weeks while the papers were finalized and the birth certificate made out – the parents hadn't been able to afford to pay for this, so in the end the birth certificate we got had our names on as parents. We got him a Brazilian passport and got on the plane home, and when we arrived mystified the immigration official who couldn't understand why we hadn't got him a British passport, assuming he was our own blood child. We just looked blank and they waved us through.

The whole business probably cost us about £5,000. I suppose that's about the price of a new car. We had fares, hotels, lawyers' fees, a fee for the baby's medical expenses. Sometimes I'm sure it's more; the lawyers charge too much, or you have to end up paying all the baby's hospital fees and so on. But, of course, it was more than all worth it – I know a child couldn't be more loved. In fact, we're going back next year to adopt a baby brother or sister for him.

Many parents who adopt from abroad cannot see that there is really any conflict of interests between their own need for a child and the child's future.

I'm absolutely sure that our son would never have lived, or that if he had, he would have been in an institution or living out of the dustbins in the streets like so many of the other children we saw in Rio or São Paulo. I know all the arguments made against intercountry adoption, most of them by armchair socialists. But we can't deal with giving aid so that in twenty years the country might be richer, we can only deal with the situation now, and the situation now is that babies like Jamie are abandoned and starving, and girls are being sold into infant prostitution. I think that *any* family, anywhere, unless there's obvious cruelty, must be better than that.

Many parents go to some trouble to make sure that the child learns about his country of origin and has pride in his background:

Fortunately, there are a lot of Indian and Pakistani children living in our area and attending the local school, so our son is able to learn from them about the kinds of families they come from, religion and so on. We've bought Indian children's books and Indian dolls and when he's older we'll make a point of taking him to exhibitions, listening to Indian music and we'll try to visit India too. I think we feel much better about it because he's not alone in this country, which he might be if someone from Germany or Scandinavia had adopted him.

While many of these adoptions work out very well for all concerned, the difficulties involved and the lack of support felt by many couples are very off-putting. Perhaps intercountry adoption will be made easier in the future, but in the meantime, it will be a very determined couple who have the confidence to try.

2

How the Child is Placed

1. Getting news of a child

Once you have been accepted by an adoption agency, there is usually a considerable wait until you are sent news that there is a suitable child for you to adopt. Again, if you are looking for a hard-to-place child, the process is likely to be shorter – you may find the child you are wanting is already waiting for you and increasingly agencies are recruiting and preparing families with a specific child in mind throughout. After being informed that the child is available, you then are sent or given details of the child, his or her background, and told of any special considerations involved in the adoption. Obviously the older the child, the more information there is going to be.

Some people find this the most difficult part of the process – being offered a real, live child, and deciding whether or not you want to go ahead with this one. This is particularly so if the child isn't quite what you had wanted.

> We were given details of a little boy of eight or nine, half chinese, very intelligent, with a photo and details of what he liked doing, his background and so on. But there had been social problems in his family, and I did want a baby. It was an agony, living with the image of this child for a whole week, opening your heart to him and really considering it. In the end we said no, which wasn't easy.

2. Detailed information

If you decide to go ahead and look into it further, you will usually have the opportunity to discuss the child further with the adoption agency worker and possibly the child's own social worker. You will probably be shown photographs of the child, and the child's background, life history, health, behaviour and

29

abilities will be explained to you as fully as possible, both the good points and the bad, so that you can try to assess whether you would suit one another. At this stage you should also get a rough idea of the time-scale involved in getting to know the child and the child coming to live with you, and also be told if there are likely to be any problems in adopting the child, for example the natural parents changing their mind. You may be given the child's whole file to read if you would like this, and will probably be asked to think about it all for a day or two before deciding that you want to go ahead and meet the child. You should also have the chance to meet the people who know the child best, be they foster parents, a housemother in an institution, teachers, or even a natural parent. In the case of a handicapped child it might also be useful to talk to the doctor or specialist who knows most about the child's condition. All this should be done before meeting the child in case anything influences you to change your mind.

3. A first meeting

Once you have decided that you do want to go ahead, the first meeting will usually be arranged as soon as possible. If you are adopting a baby, clearly the first visit is going to be very one-sided, simply for you to decide that this is really what you want and say 'Yes'. This decision isn't easy either, as these two mothers show:

> The foster mum let us in, and proudly showed us the baby, now about four months old. She loved this child, and was nearly in tears, expecting us, I think, to say 'Yes' or 'No' on the spot – but we had already decided we mustn't rush into a decision. After all, we had had years of infertility problems of different kinds, and this was an enormous change, and very, very sudden. So we went back and talked about it, but as soon as we did, we knew that if we didn't want this child, then we didn't want to adopt. So we said 'Yes'.

> We had said we would adopt a mixed race baby, so we were offered a baby fairly quickly. I had wanted a girl, and what we

were offered was a full Indian, premature baby boy. I went to the hospital to see him, trembling with nervousness, and indeed his appearance was a shock; masses of thick black hair, huge eyes that rolled back to show nothing but the whites, and he looked totally unlike us. He had been in the premature baby unit for six weeks, and he was truly odd-looking. I found it hard to say yes. But my husband responded immediately and saw him for what he was, a defenceless, extremely distressed tiny human, and as we visited him at the foster mother's, I began to feel drawn to him.

People who are adopting children often find their first reactions differ from their expectations, especially when adopting small babies. Many new natural mothers say they do not bond with their babies at first, and find them ugly, alien beings. But a natural mother – or father to some extent – has at least gone through nine months' pregnancy, the birth, and can look for similarities in the tiny newborn to themselves. The mother also has hormonal reactions and responses that will affect her. On the whole, it seems unreasonable for adopting couples to expect to fall in love at once. Also, most adopting couples have been through a long period of bereavement at not having a child of their own and this can numb their feelings when the longed-for event finally happens.

With an older child, the process is much more complex. The child is an individual who you can get to know, and who may have very strong views about the kind of parents he wants. The adoption agency worker, the child's social worker, the staff at the children's home where he or she lives or foster parents, and sometimes the natural parents may also be involved in first meetings. Sometimes a first meeting goes off well, sometimes badly. This does not usually indicate how successful the adoption will turn out to be.

When we went home after the first visit we thought, What have we done? It wasn't that Peter was more handicapped than we had thought, it was that he was so ugly – fat, pale and greasy-looking. But we felt tremendous pity and the beginnings of love and just couldn't let him down. Of course, now, no one would recognize him – he's slim, brown and much more mobile – and we can't imagine being without him.

The most usual place to meet the child is at his foster home or institution where he lives, but sometimes this is not felt to be best and the first meeting will be arranged as an outing, perhaps to a park or zoo. This meeting is likely to be the first of several, depending on the child's age and circumstances.

4. Introductory visits

Once the child seems ready, visits to the adopter's home are usually arranged – perhaps for a day, perhaps for a weekend. The number of such visits will be arranged to suit you and the child. When the time is right for the child to move in permanently with you, it is important that he says 'goodbye' properly to his past home, packs up his belongings and understands that he is never coming back. If this is not done, the child can remain confused and this will affect how he settles in to his new life.

The main aim during the introductory visits is to help the child feel ready to move – to feel that he knows the people he is going to, and that he has felt himself involved in the process, not simply been 'moved' against his will. The child needs to get to know the new parents and also release the ties he has with his foster family or staff at the children's home. The stronger these ties are, the more difficult may be the process of adjusting to the change. Contact with his past home is likely to be important for a time at least – no-one likes to be severed completely from their past friends and life. It is important that he knows that those who are presently taking care of him know about and approve of his move and gets their reassurance that this is all for the best. The new family, too, need a little time to adjust, to prepare themselves, friends and relatives, and especially other children in the family if there are any.

Sometimes the introductory visits drag out over a long time, especially if the prospective parents live a long way from the child and visits have to be carefully arranged and spaced out. This is a very insecure time in the life of any child, and there is much to be said for him moving to his new home as quickly as possible, while bearing in mind the need for him to have time to adjust. People often decide to move a child 'at the end of term' or 'after the holidays', but thought should be given to whether this is really best. It might be easier for a family to settle down during term time where there is a familiar routine and structure to the day than during the holidays. Sometimes indeed the agency's plans have to be changed because of the child's reactions.

> Joe seemed very keen to come and see us and was thrilled with his 'own' bedroom, with the toys we had bought him and especially with the garden which he loved. He also took a shine to our teenage son Mark and followed him everywhere. At the end of the weekend he didn't want to go back and made a terrible fuss, and we could only calm him down by promising he would be coming back next weekend. He kept asking to come back and in the end we had a call from the children's home saying that they thought it would be best if he came a day early, on the Friday, and we needn't bring him back if he didn't want to come, which needless to say, he didn't!

The child's sense of time is very different to an adult's – a week may seem an eternity, and six months incomprehensible. If the visits go on too long, he may become confused and wonder why his new family are delaying and keep sending him back. Most of the problems and joys of having a child will not emerge until the whole family are living together; the introductory period is bound to be strained, with everyone on their best behaviour and making a special effort. There is a lot to be said for getting on with everyday life as soon as possible.

Not all introductions go well. Some children hide their fears by a pretended indifference and a 'don't care' attitude which their prospective parents may find very hard and hurtful. Others may react by trying to put the adopters off, behaving badly and causing painful scenes. How the child behaves at this stage does not necessarily indicate the success of an adoption. Sometimes the introductory stage will take weeks and months before something clicks into place.

Claire had spent several years in and out of an institution, foster homes and one disastrous attempt to return her to her natural mother. She was extremely withdrawn, and on the first few visits would not say a word to us. We proceeded very slowly, and we got clues that she was becoming more secure in our presence, and that the repeated explanations made by the foster mother about going to a new family were beginning to sink in. She behaved as if she didn't care what happened to her, and would always say whatever she thought somebody wanted at the time, never her real feelings. The first weekend she came, we thought we were making a terrible mistake. We had three children of our own, the youngest being Jack who at eight was two years older than Claire. Without doing anything obviously wrong she just seemed to get on everybody's nerves, mainly by being so 'good'. We had our doubts about it, but my husband in particular wouldn't turn back now. Bit by bit, we saw her loosen up. One day when Jack took a toy she wanted she cried and hit him, which was the first time we had seen any real emotion from her. Now, when I look at our noisy, naughty child, I can't believe that it's the same girl nor that we could ever have had such doubts about her.

Children who have suffered emotional or physical deprivation, who have known many homes or lived for a long time in an institution, may take a very long time to settle into their new family. In fact, the child may seem much easier at first while there is still some uncertainty about its future but, once they have moved in and the parents say the child is theirs for good, begin to test them out by showing very demanding behaviour.

Many children are afraid that they will be rejected by their new family, and may start off on their best behaviour, often being irritatingly 'good' and completely unspontaneous. If mishaps occur, such as wetting the bed, or breaking something in the home, the child may try to cover it up, deny that it was their fault, and lie to protect themselves. Some children then go through a very difficult phase in which they behave as badly as possible, trying to force the parents into the rejection that they feel sure will ultimately come. Children are also testing out the limits of their behaviour; they do not know the new rules of the house, or what their new family like or dislike, and misbehaving is one way of finding out.

All of us as adults have experiences which can help us understand what the child is going through at this time. Imagine yourself staying at a house of a friend's friend in a foreign country. You have met your hosts several times, but don't really know them very well, and are not sure that they are really happy about your staying. You are not told when mealtimes are, what time you are expected to get up or go to bed, or how various things in the house work. On the first morning you spill a cup of coffee all over the bedclothes and run off all the hot water in the bathroom so that your hosts have to wash in cold water, and because you are so nervous at lunchtime you drop your plate on to the floor and break it. Your hosts are very kind and say it doesn't matter but you get the feeling that they are put out.

It can be quite important when the child is visiting to arrange simple activities and excursions which the child can enjoy – this might be a trip to a children's playground, to the local super-market, or to a place of local interest. It is a good idea not to introduce the child to too many new neighbours, friends and relatives; it is hard enough to be getting to know the family without having to try to relate to other people as well. It is also important to give the child a space of his own so that if he feels things are too much he can go there and be by himself, perhaps with a book or toy which will give him an excuse for wanting to go there.

If there are other children in the family it can be a good idea to get them to play some game together, but not one that is too complicated or too competitive. It can also help to do something that you know the child does very well, so that he can take some pride in showing off his skills and feel that he has something to offer. You don't want to make a visit a programme of non-stop activities, but you do want to avoid boredom. Also think of things that the whole family can do together, even if only watching a favourite television programme.

Often people remark of a child who has been brought up in a disorganized and traumatic family or in an institution that he has 'no interests'. The child may show no interest in joining in with anything and may simply lounge around watching television or retreat into his room for hours. Sometimes this is because the child has never had the opportunity to play, to do things with adults, or to organize his own activities. It may also be because the child lacks self-confidence and feels safer doing nothing than doing something which might expose his lack of knowledge or skills. This can be very difficult to cope with during introductory visits when you are very anxious that he should enjoy himself and that all should go well.

Adoptive parents must understand the reasons for their child's 'testing out' behaviour and know how to deal with it. Children who are to be adopted often put down the rejection or the bad experiences they have suffered to their own 'badness'. 'If I hadn't been so bad, Mummy wouldn't have sent me away.' They have to come to terms with their past; this means learning the facts and experiencing the appropriate emotions that go with them, whether they be grief, anger, pity, or loss. The adoptive family can help the child by providing a secure environment in which the child can regress and relive their experiences in a healthier way.

Many adopted children behave in a way which is normal for a much younger child. They have a great need to be 'babied' and made the centre of attention. The wise adoptive parent will allow their child to regress without fear of ridicule or rejection and satisfy some of the early needs they have missed out on. This is one reason why it often helps for an adopted child to be the youngest in the family, although that isn't always necessary. Adopted children also need a great deal of praise and re-assurance, to be told that they are lovable and good. Adoptive parents must be able to break through the vicious circle of rejection, anxiety, bad behaviour, more rejection which is behind the problems of the testing period.

5. *The probationary period*

The legal process of adoption is quite a lengthy one. You have to look after the child for a probationary period of at least 13 weeks (not including the first six weeks of a baby's life) before he or she can become a legal member of your family through the granting of an adoption order by the courts. You also have to give the local authority three months' notice that you have in your care a child who you wish to adopt. You may then have to wait some time for a court hearing, so the whole process can take many months. The procedure may be different for private or inter-country adoptions.

The local authority has a duty to supervise and 'secure the well-being' of children placed for adoption. When the court receives the application a guardian *ad litem* may be appointed to look into the adoption, interview all people concerned and make a full report to the court if there is likely to be any dispute over the adoption; otherwise, a reporting officer is nominated. During the probationary period this person, usually a social worker, will visit your home to make further inquiries. This can be nerve-wracking for prospective parents who may feel under strain at this time and fear that they are not coping as well as they had anticipated. The settling down period can be very difficult for both parents and children. Just as many parents who have given birth to a child find the first few weeks at home chaotic and strange, and may experience feelings of depression or inability to cope, so the couple looking after a baby they hope to adopt may face teething troubles. The social worker will not be trying to catch you out, but to offer advice and help, and will keep in touch till the adoption takes place.

The adoption agency worker will also keep in close touch with you, and some agencies have discussion groups for new parents which can be helpful. The purpose of the probationary period is to make sure that you, the child, and any other children in your family, can settle down to a happy life together. If you find that you have real doubts as to whether this child is the right one for you, or you the right family for them, then do raise this now, as it would be much better for the child if the agency found him or her an alternative home. The danger sign is usually a growing feeling of hostility within yourself about the child. It is not possible to love everyone, and sometimes it is better not to try. One would-be adopter describes how she and her husband decided not to go through with a placement, and how it was the most painful experience of her life:

> Daniel was rising two and at first sight a lovable, curly-haired endearing child. He babbled away to himself, spoke a few words, was very active, and we were warned about the fact that he didn't sleep much and that we would have trouble settling him into any kind of routine, and also that he had terrible tantrums. None of this worried me, as I'd had two children of my own (now grown up and away from home, one with a toddler of her own) and well remembered the tantrums and bedtime scenes! From the start, though, something just didn't go right between Daniel and me. For a start, he was incredibly physically strong, and he resisted everything, nappy changing, getting dressed, getting undressed, getting in the bath, getting out of the bath, going to bed, going out, getting in the car, eating his meals – every tiny thing became a battle of wills between us. I became mentally and physically exhausted. To make it worse, my husband found him much easier to deal with and when he came home from work he couldn't understand why I was in such a state. I discussed all this with the staff at the home where he was and they all agreed that these were problems, but somehow it didn't bother them. It was their job, I suppose, so if he was difficult or stayed up half the night it was just part of their work, and I also found out that they had given in to him a lot just to make life easier.
>
> I could have got through it all if I had felt any warmth growing in me towards this little terror. But I didn't. On the contrary, I found myself gradually coming to hate him. On many occasions I came near to really hitting him – not a sharp slap, which I confess I often gave, but a real beating. The end came when my daughter asked if I could look after her little boy for a weekend while she went away. Daniel absolutely terrorized Tom, pushing him over every time I turned my back, hitting him, stealing everything from him, and knocking him over. I instinctively went to Tom's defence every time and in the end I had this overwhelming desire just to lock Daniel in his room and leave him there, so that Tom and I could get

some peace. I realized then that I hadn't bonded with him at all, that Tom was 'my' grandchild whom I loved and that Daniel had no claim on my affections at all. It was a terrible realization. My husband and I talked it through, and when we realized that Daniel had to go, I felt the most acute guilt. I felt I had failed completely, and I hated myself for having let everyone down and for feeling nothing but hatred for this innocent child.

6. *Going to Court*

Adoption orders can only be granted by a court of law, and applications can be made to a county court or a magistrate's court or, in difficult or complex cases, to the High Court. In Scotland adoptions are dealt with in the Sheriff's Court and there is a slightly different procedure. In England and Wales adoptions are normally granted in the county or magistrate's court; the adoption agency will help with the procedure and a solicitor is not normally needed. Cases are heard privately and the proceedings are short and simple, and fairly informal. The adopters are required to be present, but not the natural parents unless they oppose the adoption, and the child does not always have to attend, especially if he is very young. The necessary investigations are all carried out beforehand and it is only in cases where the natural parents contest the adoption that proceedings become complicated and potentially expensive. In a case where the natural parents are involved because they have withheld their consent to the adoption, the courts will often go to great lengths to keep the identity of the natural parents from the prospective adopters. Even though both have to attend Court, arrangements may be made so that they never see one another.

Before the adoption order is granted the court must be satisfied that all parties involved understand the full significance of what is happening; agreement to the adoption must have been obtained from the child's parents or guardian and, if he is old enough to understand, the judge must 'ascertain the child's wishes and feelings'.

Because of changes laid down in the Children Act 1975 giving more weight to the child's needs (see Introduction, p. 4) it is now more likely that adopters may be offered a child in the full knowledge that there may be a dispute when the adoption goes to court though this still happens in only a small minority of cases. This is normally something prospective adopters would be warned about and be able to consider in advance. The agency should have sought legal advice in these cases and be fairly confident that the case could be won, and also be prepared to meet the cost. In fact, in theory any natural parent can change his or her mind up till the time the adoption is granted, even if he or she has signed the consent forms.

A contested adoption is probably the most painful aspect of the adoption process; the uncertainty can drag on for months, and the outcome is never entirely certain till the hearing is over.

When we decided to adopt Kevin it was clear that there would be a court case over it. He had gone into care on a 'place of safety' order and his natural mother never did consent to the adoption. The social workers all wanted to be as sure as they could be before going to court that the adoption would go through, so legal advice was sought and that all seemed to go on for a long time.

The case was legally very complicated and it went to the High Court. It all seemed to hinge on whether the mother was 'unreasonably' withholding her consent or not. In fact, in court we thought we had lost the case because her barrister argued that she hadn't been told about us and therefore couldn't consent, as she didn't know what she was consenting to. This took my breath away; it had never occurred to me that she wouldn't have been told something about the family Kevin was going to.

The reply to this was that she could accept 'professional opinion' that the course of action taken was the right thing for the child, so in the end – after two days in court – we heard that it had gone ahead. The relief was enormous. We knew that Kevin's situation had been horrific and that there were very good reasons for the adoption and we never felt that we were wrong in pressing to adopt him.

About three weeks after the hearing I wrote to the solicitor saying that I was concerned that the mother had not been told about us and wished that he would try to let her know the situation, that Kevin had two brothers and a sister in his new family, and that we would never say anything hostile to him about her. But I don't know whether she ever received that message.

In other cases, the issues are even more complex and the waiting period can go on indefinitely. Tessa and her husband had three children of their own and had fostered when they heard of Lucy, four and a half months old, who was mentally handicapped and had physical problems too. They had thought about adding a handicapped child to their family and decided to foster Lucy with a view to adopting her later.

Lucy had been made a ward of the High Court. Her natural mother was mentally handicapped and Lucy had been taken away from her at birth because they thought she was incapable of looking after her. The father had taken advantage of her sexually, and obviously wasn't suitable to look after the child, as he had two class one sexual offences against children. Nonetheless, he applied for custody, or at least for access, and we had three court cases in the first year Lucy was with us. The cases went against the father and it was decided that it wasn't in the child's interest for him to have access. We didn't have to go to court ourselves, but we had to talk to the court welfare officers.

We have been trying to adopt for over two years. They want to have everything cut and dried so that there's no chance at all of the case being lost when we go to court for the adoption hearing. Both parents have now agreed that it is best that Lucy is adopted and have signed all the forms, but the social services keep sending people back to check that they really understand what they're doing and haven't changed their minds. I still don't know how long it will drag on for, but if we have to go to the High Court it will be another year.

I don't think the uncertainty has hindered our bonding with

Lucy in any way. We have to explain to everyone why we haven't adopted her yet which is difficult, but we love her like the others. The worst thing is that at the back of our minds there's always the fear of losing her. It seems unjust somehow that you could lose a child who feels like yours.

'Open' adoption

One change in the way that adoptions are handled today is an increasing willingness to involve the child's natural parents and sometimes other relatives both before and after an adoption is formalized. Some parents know that they can never provide a stable home for their children, but have nevertheless kept in touch with the child while he or she was living with a foster family or in institutions. When a child is older and has more knowledge of the past, it makes sense that they may be reluctant to relinquish all ties with their old family. Adoptive parents will in some circumstances therefore be asked whether they would mind keeping in contact with the child's natural family.

Many families are very happy to keep in touch with, for instance, a child's grandmother, uncle or aunt.

We used to go and visit Sally's grandmother three or four times a year, and occasionally she would come and stay with us for a few days. I didn't find her an easy person to warm to, but she doted on Sally and could see that she was happy in her new home, so she accepted us. We used to pick up lots of fascinating – and sometimes useful – information about Sally's childhood, and there was a box of old photos which Sally loved to go through, and which gave her a sense of her past. We never found it a problem at all.

Some children have brothers and sisters now living with other families and here again keeping in touch can be of benefit to all. Where problems usually occur is where one or both of the natural parents want to keep in touch with the child. Adoptive parents, once they have formed a strong bond with their child, may fear that the natural parents will make a rival claim, even if the child is no longer legally theirs. They fear that contact with the natural parents may upset the child and set up a conflict of loyalties. Often, indeed, this is the case.

Since Annie was nine when she came to us and had always been visited by her mother, it made sense for us to allow the visiting to continue after we adopted her (she was completely in agreement that adoption was best; she was remarried and had another child and her new husband wouldn't have Annie in the house). But she was hopelessly unreliable and usually was either very late or didn't turn up at all for visits. This used to upset Annie terribly. She was much more upset than she would have been if I or her new father had been late – it was because she felt it was another rejection. The idea of her 'real' mother (we called her Annie's 'first' mother but she always preferred the former term) still held some great significance for her, and while she could intellectually understand why she couldn't live with her, she could never really accept it emotionally.

We found the whole process very distressing and, since the visits were legally at our discretion, we suggested that they stop. Annie's mother insisted that she saw the child once more, but she failed to turn up then too (we always managed to meet in a public place as we found that easier and it had poured with rain; the next day she did ring and apologize). After that she made do with letters and birthday presents, although she didn't always remember those on time either.

Sometimes contact with the natural parents does work, helps to give the child a sense of continuity, and benefits the new parents too.

John was severely handicapped, and his natural parents, who had three other lively young children and lived in cramped council accommodation, just felt they couldn't cope. They wanted to see the family that he went to before he was adopted and they wanted to keep in touch, especially for the sake of the children. We never had any doubts about this arrangement.

They visited regularly, helped us to buy things for him, never forgot his birthday or Christmas, and helped out visiting him whenever he was in hospital. They always told us that if we felt it was best for John they would drop out of our lives completely, and this really confirmed for us the fact that they put him first and did everything out of a real love for him, even though they hadn't felt able to care for him themselves. Their other children too were a joy, and we felt we got a lot out of this ready-made family!

Contact with the natural parents can cause problems, however, even when it is not intended. One mother criticizes the local authorities' policy of placing children for adoption within the area from which they came:

I don't think they realize what a small world it is here. Lucy is not supposed to have any contact with her natural father or family. But her father's niece is at the hospital under the same doctor as Lucy. We asked to be moved to another doctor or hospital but they wouldn't transfer her. Once we were there in the waiting room and I was chatting to another woman and she started to ask me lots of questions. I suddenly realized who she was and I dashed out of the room with Lucy and asked someone to get us away and cancel the appointment or there was going to be a terrible scene. I was afraid that if the father heard from his sister – I'm sure that was who it was – that she had seen us and what Lucy was like it would renew his desire to get in contact. Also, I'm afraid to go shopping in town because I know he goes there and I might bump into him or his family. People think it's silly, but it's not. I actually know a lot about Lucy's medical condition because a neighbour of mine was in the same ward having her baby as Lucy's natural mother, so she saw her then and remembered a lot of what had been said. I think it would be better, if they know the parents can't ever have the child, if they placed them further from home.

3

Children with Special Needs

Almost all adopted children, except perhaps for babies adopted soon after birth, have special needs of one kind or another. But this is a matter of degree. As more and more 'hard to place' children find families who want them, adoptive parents may have to make considerable changes to their lives to meet these needs. Handicapped children will need special equipment, perhaps special schooling, special ways of handling. Children with disturbed family backgrounds or a long history of institutionalization or failed foster placements will need special handling too.

Outsiders are often suspicious of the motives of people who want to adopt children with moderate to severe handicaps or severe behaviour problems. We place so much emphasis in society on the perfect that we find it very hard to accept that those who fall short of our ideals are also people and that they too can be loved, and can also give a great deal. One agency that specializes in very-hard-to-place children said that they never question people's motivation.

> There's an assumption that there must be something wrong with people who want to take on these children. Well, isn't there something wrong with all of us? If a couple adopt a severely handicapped and dependent child, who is always going to be dependent on them, then perhaps they are doing it because they desperately need someone to be dependent on them. But we only have to look at what happens to the children after placement to see that they thrive and that the family are happy. Part of the problem is that people won't respect other people's decisions and see that what is a burden to them is a joy to others. We should be more tolerant, we should be able to move from what we want and can do, to what others can.

Professionals today are still often suspicious of people who say

45

they want to adopt a severely handicapped child and stress only the negative aspects of such placements. It is as if they underestimate the wealth of sheer love, courage and determination in ordinary people which enables them not only to take on such a task but also to find great fulfilment in it.

What sort of people adopt handicapped or disturbed children? The studies that have been done, and the experience of adoption agencies who find homes for hard-to-place children, show that they are ordinary people, perhaps singled out by the fact that they love children, have a very child-centred lifestyle, and a great sense of fun and humour. They do not set very high expectations for the child and are delighted with the smallest progress.

One study of people who had adopted mentally handicapped children (called *Against the Odds, Adopting Mentally Handicapped Children*) found that of twenty families, only one mother worked outside the home full-time, and one part-time. The full-time working mother worked with mentally handicapped people and one of her tasks was to supervise school meals in the special school which her son attended, so even she was not far removed from him. The fact that the majority of mothers had chosen not to work reflected their commitment to parenthood. Interestingly, six fathers were unemployed and therefore also able to spend a lot of time on the children. Five were on regular shift work and at home sometimes during the day and another worked within a stone's throw of his own home.

The majority of families lived close to an extended family who also provided a lot of support, whether this was provided by parents or grown-up children; some had older children still at home. All the families were very child-centred and lived very home-based lives – the comment 'We never go anywhere without the children' came up in almost every interview. Many of these parents could not say exactly why they had wanted to adopt a handicapped child. Some were childless, others had experienced the loss of a child or had a gap in their lives made by older children leaving home. An awareness that handicapped children were unwanted by other parents was important in deciding to adopt them. Some saw looking after such a child as a challenge, and some knew that looking after a handicapped person could be

CHILDREN WITH SPECIAL NEEDS

very rewarding because they had experience of handicap already in their families or among friends. As many as seventeen of the families obviously found it so rewarding that they said they would like to adopt another handicapped child.

Practical considerations

There are many practical considerations to be taken into account when taking on a handicapped child, such as transport, special equipment, and long-term questions such as finding a suitable school, and how to cope with the handicapped teenager or young adult. Because there are so many practical issues involved which need a specialist's knowledge, most agencies who place children with severe handicaps offer a 'post-adoption' service. Instead of the 'right, now you're on your own' attitude to parents when an adoption is formalized, these agencies make sure that the parents can ring up with specific problems and get advice; some agencies ring up fairly regularly to make sure that all is going well. There are critical times when many parents need support, such as their child starting school, or their child reaching adolescence and beginning to develop sexually, and the need to find sheltered employment or special training when the child leaves school.

In most cases this post-adoption service is merely a continuation of the very careful preparation that goes on in preparing a family for the child. Any couple who adopt a child with moderate to severe handicaps will be counselled very carefully about what they can expect from the child in terms of behaviour and development and will be encouraged to think about the future. A couple may adore a Down's Syndrome baby boy, but how will they cope with a large, very backward Down's Syndrome teenager who is difficult to control and who wants to express his new-found sexual feelings? How would they cope with their boy if he also has a heart defect and a limited life expectancy?

The adoption agency also has a duty to inform and help people in claiming welfare allowances which are theirs by right if they adopt a handicapped child. The attendance allowance and mobility allowance may both be available for the parents of a handicapped child. Equipment like extra bedding, a pushchair or wheelchair, or even a washing machine may be paid for if they relate specifically to a child's special needs. The invalid care allowance is available if a parent has to stay at home to look after their handicapped child. (Married women, however, do not yet qualify for this as it is assumed that they will be at home anyway but under new government legislation married women will soon be able to claim.) A free laundry service for incontinent children and a free disposable nappy service are also provided by most area health authorities.

Parents of children with physical handicaps may need to pay for medical treatment in some cases and again they may be able to claim from the local authority or a private adoption agency may pay if they know such expenses are necessary for the welfare of the child and family.

Parents for fostered children have long received payment for the service they provide. At the time when adoption was primarily a service providing healthy babies to families, payment was obviously out of the question – in fact the 1958 Adoption Act prohibits any payment being made to couples for adopting a child. However, the Children Act 1975 proposed a trial period for subsidized adoption for certain model schemes, which came into effect in 1982. This is the 'approved adoption allowance' and is intended to help those couples who would like to adopt a child with special needs but feel unable to do so because they cannot afford another child in their family, nor the special expenses involved. The allowance may enable, for example, an un-employed couple to adopt a handicapped teenager for whom they would provide an excellent home, but who would not have been considered suitable because of their financial situation. Most local authorities now operate such schemes although they vary widely from place to place. If finance is the only thing holding you back from considering adopting a child with special needs, you should inquire at your local social services depart-ment.

These are just some of the practical issues surrounding the adoption of handicapped children. But what of the emotional ones? Many adoptive parents find it easier to bring up a handicapped child than those who have them born to them –

after all, they have chosen this, not had it thrust upon them. Natural parents of a handicapped child have first to go through a period of grief and mourning for the healthy child they thought and hoped they were going to have and who they have lost. This grief and loss may never entirely go away. Secondly, many people feel guilt for having brought an imperfect child into the world, and may feel responsible for it, remembering things they did wrong when they were pregnant, feeling they were too old to have a baby, or that there is some hereditary defect in their family which they have passed on. This makes it much more difficult for them to accept the child as he or she is, and to accept the reactions of other people to them. As one adoptive mother put it:

> Sometimes when we go shopping people look at me oddly, because they can see Tom is mentally handicapped and can't understand why I don't seem peculiar too. It doesn't bother me at all; in fact I find it rather funny, but I can see that it would bother me if he really was my own blood child.

Mentally handicapped children

A mentally handicapped person is someone who, through a hereditary condition, brain damage at birth or from accident or illness later, is limited in his or her ability to develop normal skills. Psychiatrists measure intelligence on an IQ scale with 100 as normal; anyone with an IQ of 120 or more is likely to be very bright at school and perform well in examinations and go on to higher education if they choose, and anyone with an IQ of less than 80 is considered to be subnormal. Someone with an IQ of 50 or less will be severely mentally handicapped.

One of the groups of mentally handicapped children for whom adoption is now frequently considered is those with Down's Syndrome. Babies with Down's Syndrome are almost always diagnosed at birth, so if they are rejected by the natural parents, they can be placed for adoption early. The same applies for children handicapped by hydrocephalus (water on the brain) which again is diagnosed at birth, or other birth defects, as well as brain damage caused during the birth itself. Other mental handicaps, however, may reveal themselves more slowly. A child may simply remain immature, develop slowly and show behavioural problems. Some children come from very deprived backgrounds where these handicaps are compounded by neglect; sometimes mental handicap is the result of non-accidental injury. Other mentally handicapped children have personality problems or cannot relate to people and may even be termed 'autistic' (an autistic child fails to develop the use of language or to form normal affectionate relationships with people). The later such children come into a normal family, the more severe their problems are likely to be.

Because Down's Syndrome is relatively common (one in six hundred babies born alive in Britain suffer from it), and because Down's Syndrome children are often available for adoption as babies, many people are now interested in adopting them. A Down's Syndrome child has an extra chromosome from the mother (the chromosome is the part of the cell which carries the hereditary material which dictates what the person will be like and what they have inherited from each parent). This extra chromosome causes all Down's Syndrome children to be different from the normal child, and all to have characteristics in common with one another, such as the typical Down's child's appearance with 'mongoloid' eyes, a flattened profile, sometimes stubby fingers and toes, and a low IQ (the average is about 50). Down's Syndrome children may have other problems too, such as heart defects and a limited resistance to illness, which in the past, before antibiotics and other drugs were available, meant that they often died very young. Down's Syndrome babies are usually very 'floppy' at birth, with poor reflexes, and many have difficulty with breast-feeding, as they lack the strength to suckle and often the reflexes to help them latch on. This is another reason why so many more Down's Syndrome babies live today, as they can easily be bottle-fed.

A Down's Syndrome child will develop more slowly than a normal child, but he or she will develop along a predictable pathway. Many mentally handicapped children, including those with Down's Syndrome, lack the natural drive and curiosity of normal children, which spurs them on to develop new skills. Many need pushing into achieving basic skills like sitting, walking, and using everyday objects. Many mentally handicapped children in the past were brought up in institutions where they had little stimulation and were unable to develop a strong relationship with one person, so many of their difficulties were caused by these conditions on top of the handicap, rather than the handicap alone. Many mentally handicapped children brought up in families where they receive constant affection, stimulation and rewards develop far more quickly and acquire far more skills than the professionals thought possible:

When Lucy came to us at four and a half months she did nothing. She was incredibly floppy; I remember the first time I gave her a bath I cried, because it was just like bathing a jelly. She just didn't support her limbs at all like a normal baby. Feeding was also a terrible problem; we had to force her to take anything.

She's now just over three, and I suppose her mental age is about one to one-and-a-half, except in speech – she has never said any proper words or had any normal pre-speech babble. She makes a few signs and the odd noise. She has incredible frustration tantrums – as if she's saying 'I can't do that and so I'm not going to'. We had to force her to crawl – we'd put her in a crawling position and make her move – she'd scream until it got easier, and then she learned to do it. It was the same with walking, but the trouble is, we can't *make* her talk. We can't just get hold of her mouth and move it and get the right sounds to come! But since she came to us she has improved and changed enormously and is really marvellous.

Many mentally handicapped children form very strong affectionate relationships with their new families which are very rewarding. This usually seems to be the case with Down's Syndrome children. Some show more than usual signs of attachment or jealousy:

Although my husband had had a vasectomy, which had been

reversed and not worked so we were told we'd have no more children, I got pregnant again after we had decided to adopt Lucy and she had come to live with us. When I had the baby she was terribly upset and wouldn't have anything to do with me for months.

Other mentally handicapped children may have real difficulties in relating to people, including their close family, and this can be very painful:

We did not know Patrick was mentally handicapped when we adopted him at twelve weeks old. He was a war baby and unwanted. Patrick was a very good baby, slept well, ate well, enjoyed his walks and playtimes and seldom cried.

At nine months I began to realize he was late in 'talking' and sitting up compared with other babies. At fourteen months he began to crawl and I gave him a lot of encouragement. A little friend came to play with him but they seldom made contact with one another; I wondered why. When Patrick was three I became pregnant and eventually John was born. Was it at this stage Patrick did not want to sit on anyone's lap or be cuddled? But he did not seem at all jealous of his baby brother and was happy to help with him.

I can count the hugs he gave me as a small boy when I enveloped him in the bath towel and stood him on the stool, they were so few. I will always remember those hugs and his 'I like you, Mummy'. He would never say 'I love you', though I told him 'I love you Patrick' all the time.

Patrick is now 41 years old. I feel a deep, deep sadness for him. He seems so locked up within himself and can be so selfish. He has not been a happy mentally handicapped person.

Many parents who have adopted a mentally handicapped child recall that people only put across the negative side. Adoption workers tend to be over-cautious and pessimistic about the child's achievements, perhaps to protect the child from over ambitious, unrealistic parents or the parents from disappointment if the child turns out worse than expected. In many of the cases, illustrated in the study of mentally handicapped children quoted earlier in this chapter, the parents took great pleasure in disproving almost everything the professionals had cautioned them about. The following example is a good illustration of how inaccurate some of the medical predictions about the adopted children in the study could be:

Margaret, who has cerebral palsy, was one-and-a-half years old at the time of placement. She is now five years:

Medical prediction	*What really happened*
The medical profession painted as black a picture as possible. They said she would never walk or talk or know the difference between people. They said her food would have to be liquidized. They were sure she would have epileptic seizures.	Margaret walked against all odds at four-and-a-half years. She's toilet trained day and night. She attends nursery and can make her own games. She can wash herself. She's on the borderline of going to a special school. She feeds herself; instructions to liquidize her food were abandoned one week after placement. She has never had an epileptic fit.

Physically handicapped children

Physical handicaps cover a wide range of problems, from blindness (partial or total), different degrees of deafness, and paralysis, or lack of control of the limbs and body as found with spastic children. Spina bifida is one condition found at birth where part of the spine has failed to close, so that there is a lesion below which the body is paralysed. This usually means loss of control of the lower part of the body, so that a person cannot walk and remains incontinent. Sometimes spina bifida is associated with hydrocephalus or water on the brain, in which case there may be more damage and the child may be mentally handicapped too.

Some children may lack limbs due to a birth defect; this can happen if a mother takes certain drugs during pregnancy (Thalidomide was a particularly horrific example) or if she has caught german measles (rubella) in the first three months of pregnancy. The rubella virus can also cause deafness and blindness. Other physical handicaps can be caused by hereditary diseases such as Duchenne's muscular dystrophy, where a child (usually a boy) develops normally at first but then progressively becomes paralysed, dying in young adulthood, or cystic fibrosis, an illness where the lungs become congested with a thick, sticky mucus leading to repeated infections; the pancreas also functions abnormally, preventing the digestion of proteins. The average life expectancy today for someone with this incurable disease is about twenty years.

Other genetic abnormalities can cause illness, or disfigure-ment which marks a child out from others and causes particular problems in their development. Disfigurements or disability may also be the result of a childhood accident or even non-accidental injury.

The natural parents of some of these children cannot cope with living with such handicaps or live in conditions where the help they need is not available. Others have large families and feel that they cannot cope with the extra burden involved. In any event, a number of physically handicapped children are rejected by their parents and become available for adoption.

Physical handicap is more easily understood than mental handicap and on the whole people fear it less. However, people who adopt physically handicapped children will often need an equal amount of support and face as many problems. The children will frequently need to attend special schools, and may need special equipment in the home to enable them to get around. In some cases the child's life expectancy is reduced and the parents have to learn to live with the knowledge that their child's condition is going to worsen and that they are going to have to prepare him for death. Often the children need a great deal of medical treatment and help and the families may spend a lot of time and energy on arranging for treatment, visiting doctors and hospitals and coping with the strain inevitably caused.

The positive side

The positive side of rearing a handicapped child is much more difficult to spell out than the problems, perhaps because it is much more difficult to explain about love than it is to explain about sleepless nights, messy mealtimes, dirty nappies and uncontrolled tantrums. But just as parents of ordinary children get the most enormous pleasure from seeing their children grow and develop, the personality emerge, and enjoy the romps and spontaneous events of childhood, so do the parents of handicapped children – and often more so because the pleasures are so unexpected. 'They told us she would never walk; when she took her first steps the tears just rolled down my face, I was so overjoyed. Ben, my six-year-old, was so excited he ran out into the street yelling "She's walking! She's walking!" for all the neighbours to hear.' Indeed, it is the other children in families where a handicapped child was adopted who often reveal those pleasures much more accurately than the parents.

Adoption agency workers often worry about the effect that a handicapped child will have on other members of the family where there are older children. Again, the study quoted on page 46 shows that usually there is no need to worry. Some of the older children in this study had some initial fears about adopting a handicapped child, mainly because they did not understand what handicap was about and imagined some kind of monster. These fears faded when they saw the actual child. (As one 11-year-old boy put it: 'When I first heard of her I thought "What are we laying on ourselves now?" But when I saw her I thought the opposite. When I met her she just fell for me as her brother'.) When asked to describe their handicapped brother or sister, they gave lively descriptions of each child's quirks and charms. Almost all of these were positive. When presented with a sheet of words and asked to circle the ones which described the handicapped child best, 'quick' and 'clever' were frequently picked, while words like 'odd' or 'different' were usually ignored. One mother describes her children's reactions as follows:

> Our children were twelve, eight and seven when Lucy came to live with us. They were involved from the very start and consulted all the way – they took to her at once and were impatient for her to be their little sister and to bring her home. They knew about her special needs and that she would be 'different' but accepted, and still accept, her for herself. They help look after her, are aware that she needs more watching and looking to than other children and they help when they are able when asked – and sometimes when not asked. I am sometimes astounded by how attentive they are to Lucy – I thought the novelty of having a little sister would wear off sooner!

The fact that children of families who adopt handicapped children seem to feel proud rather than ashamed of their handicapped brother or sister probably reflects their parents' own attitudes. In this study, fears for the children's welfare were certainly unfounded. As the study concluded, while professionals spent many anxious hours addressing the question, 'How much will the siblings suffer?' it never occurred to them that it might have been more appropriate to ask, 'How much will the siblings benefit?'

Most people who have adopted a handicapped child say the rewards are tremendous.

> She has given us something very special, we feel we understand what is important in life now and what isn't. Don't ever let anyone tell you it's easy – it's probably the most difficult thing I've ever done in my life. But then, it's always the difficult things that give you the most pleasure. Of course, I've had my times when I've been down, when nothing's gone right, when I've worried about her future and what she'll do when we're not around. But we've also laughed – my goodness, haven't we laughed!

Older children

The majority of people wanting to adopt would probably choose a baby first, then if possible a pre-school child. The older a child becomes, the less likely people are to want to adopt them. Agencies who find homes for hard-to-place children say that the greatest obstacles faced by them are their age and sex. On the whole, people want young children, and the majority of adopters want girls, especially when considering older children. Why this is so has never been clear; more boys than girls also end up in care, perhaps because people see them as being less affectionate and harder to manage, the same reasons for which adopting parents might prefer to have a daughter.

Age is a problem because some people fear that, unless they get the child young enough, his personality will already have been formed and he can never be 'theirs' in the sense that they would like. Older children will inevitably have memories of life before they came to live with their new families, and perhaps a stronger attachment to their natural parents or to foster families, which new parents might find threatening. If the children have been in care for a long period, have moved from their natural families into care and back or had a series of foster homes the child is likely to be emotionally damaged and to have all kinds of behaviour problems which make them unattractive candidates for adoption. In addition, many of these older children have brothers and sisters from whom they do not wish to be separated, so that adopters would have to take on a ready-made family.

These children do need homes however, and as late in their lives as adolescence can benefit from having a permanent family to live with and provide a stable base from which they can go out into the world. Adopting teenagers, however, is comparatively rare as the majority of much older children are likely to be found foster homes.

A considerable number of older children who are available for adoption have behaviour problems, and many also have poor health or are very backward in development. Some show destructive or aggressive behaviour or are very withdrawn, and have problems such as bed-wetting, soiling, speech problems, and are difficult to manage. Many show a very shallow emotional response and have difficulty in relating either to adults or to other children.

Parents who take on children with these problems are obviously asking a lot of themselves and their families. Sometimes, after a period of very difficult behaviour in which the child acts out his fears of abandonment or anger at what has happened to him and the grief of losing his natural parents, the child will settle down and make enormous strides. This does not always happen, however, and some children appear unable to recover and form close relationships with their new families:

> Claire came to us at six after a very deprived infancy. Her first weeks of life were spent in an incubator and her inadequate mother abandoned her to her landlady and husband who was alcoholic. The social services eventually removed her and she spent two years in a children's nursery before being placed with us for adoption.
>
> She remained very shy and also had the most terrible outbursts of temper where she was very destructive. In the twelve years she has been with us I have never heard her refer to the past or the future. She knew how to provoke us and how to get under our skin and force us to dislike her. I fear that she is unable to make meaningful relationships.

Other very disturbed children can have a catastrophic effect on other children in the family, especially if the children are younger (for this reason many adoption agencies specify that the child you adopt must be the youngest in the family though this is now changing as experience shows that successful adoption follows no rules). The child's aggression and difficult behaviour can be taken out on the other children. 'At first my two daughters begged us to take him back. Their toys were broken, their books torn, their private space invaded. Daniel would scream when they were trying to watch something on television and say terrible things to all their friends. But we told them he wasn't going and that was it – eventually it settled down.' Not all such situations have a happy outcome, though, and prospective parents and the adoption agency should be aware of the potential problems to try to prevent situations like the following disaster:

> We had one child but I was unable to have any more, and since we didn't want Andrew to be an only child, decided to adopt. We considered a handicapped child, but said we would also take an older, 'hard-to-place' child. After a few months we were offered Rachel. She was six, Andrew was three, and we went carefully into the issue of how he would be affected. Rachel was a pretty girl and was on her best behaviour in the early visits, so we thought all would be well. The problems began as soon as she actually came to live with us.
>
> Andrew was jealous of Rachel, as we expected, but he was also very confused because he kept calling her his 'little sister'. Of course she wasn't little, she was twice his size and she was very aggressive towards him. We did everything we could to protect him while trying to be fair, and she did really hurt him. She would pinch his cheek so hard it left a mark for days and pushed him downstairs. Andrew became very upset and began to regress in his behaviour. He started to wet the bed frequently and to soil his pants. He started to refuse to go to his playgroup and everyone there noticed the change in him. We were still determined that Rachel wasn't going back and told him so, but things just went from bad to worse.
>
> I became depressed and overwhelmed by guilt, my mother threatened terrible things if we didn't remove Rachel, and Andrew's life became a misery. When the time came for the adoption to go to court I told the social worker everything that was on my mind and said I didn't think I could go through with it unless things improved, so we put off the hearing for another trial period. Things got better, but not much. I am still hanging back from making the final decision because I can't quite bring myself to commit ourselves – although I feel the damage to Andrew is done now and wouldn't necessarily be helped by taking Rachel away.

The institutionalized child

Most children available for adoption nowadays are likely to have spent time in foster homes rather than institutions. However, some children, particularly older ones, may have spent most of their remembered lives in an institution and be unsure how to adapt to the real world. Most residential care workers change jobs fairly frequently and there is a high turnover of staff in homes; also different people will be working different hours, so that a child will have a large number of adults caring for him or her throughout the time he is living in a home.

Many such children have problems relating to adults, in forming close relationships and adapting to family life. They are likely to be either very possessive or indifferent to personal possessions and to be materialistic, placing value on objects instead of feelings. Many children have known an inflexible routine every day of their lives and find it hard to relax in the more casual atmosphere of a family. Some lack basic knowledge about everyday life such as shopping and buying food, the work involved in preparing meals, the fact that parents are on duty 24 hours a day and seven days a week and need some rest. All these points are shown up well in the following couple's experience:

> We were astonished when Sam came to live with us not so much by the major problems, such as his lying, stealing and unsociability, but by all the little things he couldn't grasp. He didn't understand about possessions, that some things belonged to him and some to his brother, or about pocket money and how to spend it. He was intensely materialistic, and never spent his money on anything but himself; he did not seem ashamed that at birthdays or Christmas he had nothing to give us while we gave things to him. We tried to explain about gifts and gave him money and went with him to buy them, but it didn't work; he just wanted everything for himself and didn't understand the pleasure we got from giving.
>
> He couldn't work out either that the food which was always in the house was not all to be eaten when he liked; he would raid the biscuit tin and the fridge and then we'd all find there

was no milk for breakfast or nothing for tea. He didn't understand that clothes needed washing and mending and expected a constant supply of clean things. He got nervous if meals didn't appear exactly on time and got upset by changes in our routine, for instance when friends came. He also found it hard to realize that he couldn't play one of us off against the other as he used to the staff in the residential home. He was also unable to make even minor decisions, as these had always been made for him before, and asking him what he wanted to do would throw him into a panic.

Adoptive parents obviously need a lot of patience to see the child through the difficult period of adjusting to life within a family and to make the necessary allowances. Most, however, are rewarded in time by seeing their confused and difficult child turn into a more confident and well-adjusted person:

The best thing is when I peep into his room at night and see his clothes all in a heap, his books and toys all crammed into his bed and his light still on. He used to have everything so neat, lie flat on his back with the sheets pulled up to his chin and not be able to go to sleep till all was total quiet and darkness.

The 'unbonded' child

People who adopt older children often have some concern as to whether the child will ever really 'bond' with them. Children who have spent some time in institutional care often behave in a very characteristic way, being over-friendly with strangers or any adult who shows an interest in them and not showing a particular attachment to one person. Barbara Tizard's study of children adopted after some years in institutional care, *Adoption: A Second Chance*, showed that while most older adopted children were 'too friendly' with strangers and acquaintances, which often caused their parents worry, they did form a strong bond with their new parents too. It seems quite rare for a child not to do so, though it can sometimes happen:

We adopted Alice at the age of seven. Several months after she had come to live with us we went to a big department store to get a new washing machine, and she ran off and disappeared. She was found by a staff member and taken up to the information desk and they put out a call asking her parents to go there, which I did. But apparently she had been completely untroubled by being lost. The shop assistant with her had kept asking 'Is that your Mummy?' every time a likely-looking person came into view, and she would nod and say 'Yes'. The assistant was very puzzled. She felt, and I honestly believe, that she would have gone off with anyone.

How and when adoptive children and parents bond with one another is probably different in every case, but then most natural parents would accept that they do not bond with their children at birth in some mystical way. They accept that they gradually come to love their children as they live with them and care for them, and the same of course holds true for adoptive parents. Indeed, if the blood bond always guaranteed love, commitment and care, children would not ever be in need of adoptive and foster families.

The issue of whether the child can bond with his new family is closely related to whether the parents can bond with him. Indeed, most parents say that their bonding to the child is more-or-less dependent on the child bonding with them; unless they receive affection and response, the parents cannot find it easy to love the child.

Claire gave us nothing. I became aware of my lack of feelings for her, and tried to cuddle her, but being unused to physical contact, she would sit rigid and then wriggle off my knee. I was ashamed of my intense irritation with her because her conversations were so limited – and about totally trivial things.

To friends, neighbours and relatives she appeared to be charming, attractive, helpful, willing, co-operative and to create no problems, especially alongside her noisy, demanding and demonstrative younger sister. Yet hardly a day passed without Claire producing a problem situation inside the family. She seemed to know how to spoil a happy day, provoke irritations that could not be ignored, lose, break or destroy her own or family belongings and refuse to explain her own actions, always saying 'I don't know'. Trying to ignore her irritating behaviour would only lead to its getting worse and then an inevitable scene ending in some sort of punishment. Punishment had no effect on her, she never cried, and it only led to splits and disagreements in the family as to how we should deal with her.

Now, looking back, I am sorry that I didn't fully understand the signs of rejection and lack of mothering which she had suffered making it difficult for her to make relationships. We were all deeply committed to Claire but I often wondered if we were the right family and if she would have been happier in a less articulate and active family. We looked for help but found it difficult to get professionals to understand our problems.

What to do with a child who seems unable to show any affection or develop strong relationships is a worry for many parents, who fear that the children will grow up unable to make deep and lasting relationships, find a partner and bring up children of their own in a secure way. Some parents find that after a long time together, the bond begins to grow. Others find that it does not, and have to admit that their relationship with the child is one of commitment rather than love.

I realized that nothing was going to change. I just hoped that the experience of living in a stable family would be of some benefit to him in the future, even though I don't believe he really feels he belongs to us.

Such experiences are, in fact, comparatively rare for adoptive parents. Barbara Tizard's study shows that in all but one case the adoptive parents believed that their children returned the affection they felt for them; this was much greater than for children returned to their natural parents. But still, a number of adopted children remain unbonded to their families and

adoptive parents and professionals are unsure of how to deal
with this problem.

Holding therapy

One controversial therapy which has recently been tried out is
'holding therapy' – where the unbonded child is forced into a
crisis of intimacy with the parents – a therapy which was started
to try to help autistic children. The child is held against its will by
the parent and helpers and allowed to go through a whole cycle of
rage and anger until his or her fury is all spent. Young children
frequently scream and struggle furiously, older children try to
avoid making contact by laughing or shouting insults. But
eventually all the child's anger is spent and, in the calm which
follows, the parent strokes and soothes the child and then finally
lets go. The child's instinctive response is then to put its arms
around the parent.

The theory behind this is that the child, deep down, wants to
be held and comforted despite the distance he has created as a
protection against hurt and rejection. It is very difficult for
anyone to force intimacy on someone else in this way, as we
instinctively respect someone's wishes to be left alone, even if we
suspect that this desire is not the deepest one there is. This is why
many people caring for an unbonded child fantasize about some
extreme situation, such as a severe illness, an accident or fire, in
which they can come really close to the child. This therapy is not
yet widely used for adopted children and some professionals
remain sceptical about its usefulness or fear it is potentially
damaging. Some parents who had tried it, however, find it
undoubtedly works: 'I wish we'd tried it earlier. I already feel
much closer to her'.

Adopting teenagers

Adopting teenagers has its unique problems and rewards. The
normal teenager is establishing his or her own identity and
beginning to move away from the family, to reject some of their
parent's values and begin to step out on their own. All this is

rather difficult to do, however, if you haven't got a family to react against, and are still in need of the security you have missed out on. Adopting teenagers, then, means treading a delicate path between providing a stable base and letting go, and it brings out many of the problems faced by ordinary parents of teenagers in a more dramatic form.

Sarah came to us at fifteen arriving with ankle-length socks and sucking her thumb and so in need of parents that she called us 'Mummy' and 'Daddy' from the first day. She adored my husband – for the first time in her life she had a safe father-figure – she would often sit on his knee and cuddle him. With me she was more difficult – she was testing me out, trying to see where the boundaries were. From the ages of fifteen to eighteen everything was fine. Oh, she stole things sometimes, she smoked, and so on, but nothing very serious. At eighteen she went completely off the rails. She went from being very clean and neat at home to going off and living in dreadful squats. We tried to arrange a hostel for her since she didn't want to come back here but she refused, disappeared, and got into trouble with the police. At this stage we were advised that there wasn't much we could do, so we left her to get on with it.

She came back when she was four months pregnant – she was in a remand home. She wanted to have the baby and had formed a stable relationship with the child's father – they are still very much together. They had the baby and Sarah matured overnight. She went out to work and the father brought the baby up – he was a wonderfully caring father, and the child is very secure and bright. I feel that we did the right thing in 'letting go' of Sarah. Parents of teenagers, whether their own or adopted, have to set the boundaries for what they will accept and help the child to stay or leave, whatever is appropriate.

Many teenagers indeed will be looking for a stable base rather than parenting in the usually accepted sense, which is why foster homes may seem more appropriate. Children may not have become available for adoption till their teens for many reasons, but it is quite likely that they have had continued contact with their natural parents while in foster homes or institutional care, and thus may not be looking for a substitute mother and father so much as some adult friends and a home which they know will always be there to come back to. Some, however, will have had a long period in an institution and failed foster placements due to their difficulties and are desperately in need of families.

There are some particular problems in dealing with teenagers, especially those who have had unhappy childhoods. Many will lie, cheat and steal, and there are the usual problems about turning up for meals, letting the rest of the family know where they have gone and when they will be back, and the problems connected with inviting other friends back to the home and going out to late parties. There can be arguments over issues like smoking, drinking, girl- and boyfriends, and worries about early sexual relationships.

Teenagers are also expensive; they want to wear the latest fashions, go out to films, discos and eating places, and may have expensive hobbies too. Children from disorganized families and unsettled backgrounds or who have spent a long time in institutions may be very materialistic and also careless of personal possessions. It is very galling repeatedly to spend a lot of money on much-wanted clothes and equipment and then find that they have been damaged or lost.

Teenagers vary in their ability to make decisions and be responsible for themselves and others; indeed, the same teen-ager may change in this from day to day. It is important to try to involve a teenager in your care in laying down house rules, making decisions about holidays, schoolwork and how many evenings a week the teenager may go out.

Of course, at first Martin, who was 16 when he came to us, used the house like a hotel. He was hardly ever in, never told us where he was going, lay in bed for hours in the morning, ate enormous quantities of food whenever he chose but seldom at mealtimes. I remembered that our own children were just the same at that stage, but what worried us was that Martin found it hard to relate to people and he just wasn't forming any ties with us at all; he was also doing very badly at school, despite the fact that he desperately wanted to stay on and do a computer studies course. So we put it to him: he could stay as a lodger, or as a member of the family. He chose to be a member of the family, and that meant being in at least three evenings a week; taking meals when he was in with us; letting us know where he was going and introducing us to his friends; doing some of the chores and letting us help with his homework. Bit by bit it worked, and I now feel that he has gained a lot from being with us, sharing some of his worries, and getting support to help him through school, and we have gained from having him.

Problems also come when the teenager decides that it's time to leave home. Parents who have only had a child in their family for a year or two may find it hard to accept that their 'child' wants to leave and interpret this as failure on their part. They may hang on to their teenager, feeling that he or she has had an unhappy background and really needs them. This is often true, but it is impossible to force dependence on an older teenager, and sometimes parents would do better to accept and help their charge towards the independence they seek. Sometimes leaving home can be a very positive step, and a sign that the adoptive parents have successfully helped the teenager to make that difficult step from child to adult.

4

Adopting Ethnic Minority or Mixed-race Children – Transracial Adoption

Transracial adoption has become one of the most controversial areas of adoption today. In the 1960s, when the number of children adopted reached its peak, 'hard to place' children included black and mixed race children. Today this is no longer the case; as there are so few healthy white babies for adoption, people are happy to be able to adopt healthy black babies. However, it is now increasingly felt that these children should be adopted into families of the same race, rather than by white couples. It is now believed, as outlined by BAAF in a recent report, that in a black family the child has a better chance of growing up with a positive sense of racial identity, of being proud rather than ashamed of being black and better able to cope with being black in a white society in which skin colour has a major impact on life chances and experiences.

Black children form a higher proportion of children in care than their numbers in the community would lead you to expect. Recent research has shown that in some London boroughs 40, 50 and even 60 per cent of the children in care are black. This is because black people tend to be allocated the worst housing, find the greatest difficulty in finding jobs and have the lowest pay when in work. Black families also suffer greater social upheaval. This is partly because of the discrimination against black people in our society, and also because many families have been split up by immigration, by social tensions and by lack of money. Children may be taken into care because their housing is inadequate, because they are homeless, because the mother cannot afford a childminder when she goes to work, because she has no other relatives to support her. Where living conditions are so miserable, the normal tensions of everyday life may even erupt in violence. White social work agencies have also perhaps been less able to provide the kind of support needed to keep black families together and have been more ready to take black children into care.

Up till recently most black families have not had the resources to adopt children. One well-educated black social worker, taken into care herself as a child for a short period, laughs: 'You're kidding, we had our children taken into care, never mind giving us other people's kids to adopt!' Adoption has been very much a middle-class preserve, and until very recently there has been no black middle-class. Black couples approaching adoption agencies felt – often rightly – that they were treated with suspicion. There were hardly any black social workers working in adoption agencies – today there are still far too few. Adoption agencies had developed a response which was bureaucratic, off-putting, and sometimes seemed punitive. Black couples felt that they were being discriminated against:

> We got as far as the social worker coming round to see our home. It was clear she didn't like what she saw. She wrinkled up her nose looking at the food in the kitchen and she didn't like the decor in our house. I just knew we wouldn't get any further when I saw her stuffy white face at the door, but we went through this interview, all these questions. She didn't seem interested to ask us what we would do with a child, what plans we'd have for him. Just kept asking questions about our childhood and parents and whether I thought I would keep my job.

In these circumstances, it was hardly surprising that few black couples came forward offering to adopt children. Most agencies never bothered even to look for them. So most black children were placed in white, middle-class families of the sort then considered most suitable. Some of these were young, 1960s radical couples who were making a conscious gesture towards a more integrated society – adopting black children fitted well into the current 'melting pot' theory of race relations which held that race didn't matter and that integration was best achieved by mixing up different races together. Others just wanted a child and didn't mind what colour or background they were. Others really wanted a white child but were prepared to take black as second best. These children were described as 'hard to place' and many people in fact took on black children in the same spirit as they would have taken on a handicapped child.

A study of such adoptions which had taken place in the 1960s was carried out by the British Adoption Project. This study, called *Adoption and Race*, looked at the children when they had reached their teens. The study showed that by many criteria the children were doing very well – they were happy at home, got on well with parents, brothers and sisters, and were doing well at school. But the study also showed that many were the only black children in their class, that most had no black friends, and that they didn't really consider themselves as black. In fact, they talked about black people with white people's stereotypes. Asked to describe themselves, thirteen of the thirty-six children made no reference at all to colour; nineteen described themselves as 'brown' or 'coloured' and not one as black. As many as thirty out of the thirty-six did not want to live as they thought West Indians and Asians did when they grew up; this was perhaps not surprising when only four sets of parents said they were making a positive effort to give their children pride in their racial background.

The greatest concern felt about these findings was that these children would have a great shock when they left the security of their white, middle-class environment and went out into the world. How would they cope with racial prejudice when applying for jobs or making their first serious relationships? How would they cope with being seen as black by everyone else when they see themselves as white? How would they cope when they have black children of their own?

Barbara Tizard's study of adopted children, called *Adoption: A Second Chance*, showed that the majority of those who had adopted black children did not have positive feelings about the child's background. Some parents even had racist attitudes, while claiming to be unprejudiced. One mother in the study, for example, said:

There are certain traits in his character which are definitely the traits of a coloured person. There's his lack of concentration. Also, he'll suddenly switch off if he thinks you're going to tell him off – you can tell by his eye – he'll just go into his own little world. This is a thing that the coloured races do – one notices these little things.

Half the children had still not been told by the age of eight that they were of mixed race and their skin colour was never mentioned. This was clearly disturbing for the children, one of whom had developed an aversion to black people when they appeared on television. Another made black friends and was ashamed to bring them home because they would then see that his parents were white. Only one mother felt that she had a responsibility to give the child knowledge of and pride in his black ancestry. Some of the parents tried to minimize the problem by saying 'You're only coffee-coloured', and others found difficulty in explaining that the child's father was black because it involved telling the facts of life.

These findings are disturbing, and have led many working for adoption agencies to question the wisdom of placing black children with white families at all. It has certainly made them aware of the need to find ways of reaching prospective black parents in the community. In order to do this, it was clear that there should be more black social workers dealing with adoption, especially in key posts in agencies where policies are made, and in family finding and child placement. Social workers in general should become much more aware of the positive things members of the black community have to offer as parents. One early attempt to recruit black parents was the Soul Kids Campaign, which was carried out in London in 1975–76. The campaign was not a success, recruiting only seventeen black families over many months but it did give a lot of publicity to the issue, and many lessons were learned from this campaign. More recent initiatives have shown that there is, in fact, no real problem in finding suitable black families, once agencies are aware that they make the best families for their children and have overcome their own prejudices.

Nobody has suggested that children already placed in white families should be taken away, although some parents who have adopted one black or mixed race child express anger that they may not be able to adopt another, as they feel this further isolates the existing child and deprives him or her of a brother or sister. People who have adopted black children express some misgivings about the new philosophy; they feel they have been cheated.

Ten years ago they were desperate for us to adopt – we took two brothers, aged four and two, both half West Indian. Now we know they disapprove of us. We went back to the social services department saying we wanted to adopt another child and you wouldn't believe the things they said to us; in fact it upset me so much we didn't go ahead though I know we'd give a child a good home. The boys are happy and thriving and doing well at school. They've got both black and white friends and they don't seem screwed up by their background at all and they're certainly not ashamed of being black.

Many white parents of black children are sensitive to the problems and express concern about it. It does seem that many black or mixed race children in white families experience difficulties in accepting their skin colour and their background. Some children go through a stage of wanting to be white or denying their skin colour. 'Our adopted Pakistani daughter says she hates being brown, although I have to say, she says anything that will get a rise out of people, as that does.' Others don't understand why they are teased and called names like 'Sambo' or 'Nig-nog' at school. 'He came home from school the other day and said, "Why do they call me a nig-nog. I'm not am I?" ' Other parents find that they do have difficulties helping their children come to terms with the race issue:

Oh, we're painfully aware of our shortcomings. We adopted two half West Indian children, Ruth as a baby, and Kevin at three. Where we live is a very white area, and I'm sure it would have been easier in another situation. In fact, when they were small we spent four months in America in an academic community and it was fantastic. There were a lot of black people among friends and the community, no prejudice was ever expressed, and I'm sure it would have made for a happier childhood.

We did try to get a local Harmony group going here (Harmony is an association for racially mixed families) but the kids hated it. It was rather artificial – a 'there are only a few of us so let's get the kids together' attitude – and it didn't really work. We had decided to send them to the local neighbourhood school, which was quite rough. I suppose we made a conscious decision not to protect them – we may regret that. Soon after Kevin arrived I remember putting him to bed and he told me 'Some children called me Brownie today'. Ruth put her arm around him and said, 'Never mind, when you get to school they'll say that every day'.

Ruth's attitude does sometimes worry me. We invited a (white) South African to dinner one evening and afterwards Ruth confessed to me that she had been very worried in case the lady was black. We have a Jamaican friend who tries to raise her consciousness a little, but she doesn't take to it. Then she wanted to have her hair straightened so that she could 'do things with it'. I think she just wants to look like her friends.

We have done what we can to make them proud of being black. We tell them they're beautiful, which they are. Ruth's favourite book was one of West Indian stories, and we try to be with black people. But in this society we are so limited.

Many adopters of black children find that their children seem to resent attempts to interest them or involve them in black culture. Quite often this may be in the same way that children resist attempts to 'get them interested' in something parents think will be good for them, such as a sport, music, or joining a club. Others, however, may do so because they have picked up on the fact that black people suffer prejudice and discrimination in this country. If their adoptive parents have any hidden misgivings about their children's colour or about, for example, the accusations of white racism made by black groups, the children are bound to pick up on it and feel uncomfortable. This is rather similar to the position of children who 'do not want to know' that they are adopted.

Telling children about their background and helping them to be proud of being black is something which must permeate every aspect of everyday life, not just come up every now and then when children appear worried or parents feel concerned about the issue. Many parents do this very well – and it can take a surprising amount of research to find out all you need to know.

> We were determined to do the right thing by our adopted, Anglo-Caribbean daughter, so we went to the local library to find books with black people in them, information about the fight against slavery and other material we thought she would like to see. We got a map of the world from Oxfam which shows the Third World areas in their proper perspective and we went to London to find a shop that sold black dolls. But things like having her hair done were difficult! It took quite an effort to find somewhere that did Afro hair. We picked up a beauty magazine and it was full of ads for hair care products, skin care creams and make-up specially for black people which I never knew existed. Suddenly I began to realize, with some humility, that in some ways we weren't the best family for Judy, that there was so much we didn't know about. I never felt really confident, for example, in doing Caribbean cooking, though I felt it was important for Judy to know about it and she loved to help me cook. I think she picked up on the fact that I felt uncomfortable and always said she preferred English food.

Providing for a black child's physical needs is one thing, but other needs are more difficult. Many parents of ethnic minority children are concerned above giving their child some understanding of the religion they would have been likely to be brought up with had they remained in their own families or culture. But giving a child a theoretical knowledge of Hinduism, Islam, Rastafarianism or Seventh Day Adventist Christianity is very different from regularly attending a temple, mosque or church. Most parents will not be able to make such a commitment and many may disapprove of that religion or religion in general and feel it is completely inappropriate. Sometimes schools with a large ethnic minority intake may have special links with community groups and have special classes on, for example, Indian culture or Indian dance. Others may do mother-tongue teaching, which could give your child a chance to learn his or her natural parents' language. However, these are only options if you are living in a racially mixed area.

Many white parents of black children find it hard to accept the degree of racism within British society, or, if they do, to feel themselves in any way a part of it. If their children show signs of developing 'radical' ideas and politics they can feel very threatened. It is important that anyone who has adopted or may adopt a black or mixed race child faces up to their feelings and examines them carefully. It is not good enough just to answer your child by saying 'I'm not racist – I wouldn't have adopted you if I was, would I?' It is quite possible to love a black person and yet still hold racist attitudes towards black people at large.

5

Telling and Tracing:
Special Issues in Bringing Up
Your Adopted Child

In most ways, bringing up an adopted child is like bringing up your own. The important differences come in explaining to the child what adoption means, what their background is, how you came to choose them, and, when the time comes, helping them to trace their natural parents if they decide to do this. Adopted children may also carry with them more insecurity from the past than naturally born children, with a greater than usual fear of rejection, and may need to be handled with extra care and respect. This is particularly true for children who have had bad experiences in earlier childhood.

Telling the child about his or her past is now something adoptive parents are recommended to do from the outset, whether the child comes to them as a baby, toddler, or school age child. Recent research in America has shown that pre-school children understand very little of the meaning of being adopted. Long and complicated explanations at this stage are simply likely to confuse a child. It helps the children, and the parents too, however, to get used to using the word 'adopted' so that the child is used to hearing it. One mother of a toddler used to say things like: 'Oh, you are a clever boy! I'm so glad we adopted you', long before he could understand what she meant, so that he would associate the word 'adoption' with love and praise.

Once a child becomes old enough to understand a little, or to ask what 'adopted' means, the parents can begin to explain. An explanation could consist of telling the child that their first mother gave birth to him, and that he grew in her tummy, but that the first mother could not look after him for some reason, so he was given to you to bring up as your own. It can be very important for some parents to bring in the idea of choosing a special child, as this helps give the child an idea of being wanted, indeed of being uniquely chosen.

When we adopted Sam at the age of three we talked a little to the social worker about how we would tell her about her past. She had no memory of her mother, and had lived in a children's home and then with a foster family for a year. It seemed so difficult to explain about all these mothers, her natural mother, her foster mother, and then me. So to begin with we just told her how we couldn't have a baby of our own, but that we so much wanted a little girl that we had gone to choose her. We talked about her foster mother as 'Jo'. When she was a little older we decided to tell her about her natural mother but she wasn't very interested and just kept asking if I was her 'real' mother, to which I told her I was, as the 'real' mother was the one who loved and looked after a child. This seemed to be the answer she wanted.

Other families make the story of the child's choice a special one which they repeat to the child when asked; how they wanted a little boy, how they went to the children's home and picked him, how he came home with them in the car, and so on. This can be done in the same way that naturally born children hear of 'when they came home from the hospital'.

Many parents find real difficulties talking to a child about the past because it involves giving the facts of life at an early age. One parent in Barbara Tizard's study, quoted on page 61, put it like this:

So she said, 'You didn't have me in your tummy, then? Why couldn't you have a black baby?' I said, 'Because I wasn't married to a black man'. 'Do you have to be black to have a black baby?' I said, 'No, but it does help if one of you is black'. It's very awkward for a kiddy to try to understand these things.

Parents may find it difficult to explain why the natural mother could not bring up a child – he or she is unlikely to understand about illegitimacy, and telling a child that his father ran off may not be very helpful for him. Many parents of adopted children are hampered by not knowing anything about the natural father. Reasons like 'Your mother had to give you away because she was very poor' may serve, but a child might wonder if he would be given away again if his own family became very poor. In the end, there is nothing for it but to give the truth as closely as possible, gradually building on it as the child gets older. If you give the child a false story to make it easier for him at the beginning, it is going to be very difficult for him to believe what he is told later on.

Some parents know that the child was not alone, and that there were other brothers and sisters in the family. Sometimes these too were adopted, sometimes they remained with the natural parents, and this can be very hard to explain.

Ruth used to talk about being adopted a lot – it was hard for her. She used to wonder a lot about her first mother, and it had to come out that there were older sisters. I shall encourage her to trace her sisters when she's old enough.

Some parents find it so hard to tell their children that they delay, and as they delay find it increasingly difficult to come out with the truth. It is almost inevitable that an adoptive parent will have to tell, and it is far better if the child knows long before they reach the difficulties of adolescence, when they will be having enough changes to face and will be discovering their own identity. If you do not tell, you will almost certainly have to lie at some stage, and a healthy relationship with a child cannot be built on lies and evasions, certainly not about a subject so important to the child. One mother guiltily remembers:

Lisa was eight, and I was having coffee at a friend's house with her daughter and another mother. The other mother was expecting her second baby and, of course, the talk got round to hospitals and childbirth and labour. I had never told anyone that Lisa was adopted, and I always dreaded this kind of conversation. Lisa was sitting on my knee, and my friend asked, what was her birth like? So I said, 'Oh, perfectly normal', but I blushed to the roots of my hair and I'm sure she noticed. Then Lisa took it up, 'What hospital was I born in, Mummy?' So I said, 'The Northern' (fortunately, I knew). The conversation then got round to breast-feeding, and I said that I couldn't feed Lisa, she was bottle-fed. Well, you know the looks of disapproval you get for that these days!

On the way home I felt terrible and decided that we would have to tell Lisa. To my surprise, it came up very easily. Lisa told me a few days later that 'Caroline didn't come out of her Mummy's tummy. She told me she was adopted'. I took a deep breath and said, 'Well, that's just like you. Your first mummy couldn't keep you because she was very young and her family wouldn't let her, and they knew how much we wanted a little baby, so you were given to us as our very own'. To my immense relief she was not shocked, only very interested. Now I feel as if an immense weight has been taken off my mind, and a few days later I told my friend as well.

Children are very sensitive to evasions and half truths, and if they sense that you are in some way ashamed of the fact that your child is adopted, the child too will develop a sense of shame about his or her past. Many children who sense their parents are uncomfortable with the issue will resist talking about it and never ask questions, as they may fear that shameful facts will come out. Closely related to telling the child about adoption is the issue of whether to tell friends, school, neighbours and other people. If you have adopted an older child, or a child who is of mixed race, it will be obvious to most outsiders that the child is not your own. Some parents feel that it is not appropriate to tell everyone and explain to the child that this is a very special family secret, not to be told to just anyone, but only to very special people. Usually it is necessary to tell the school, especially if the child has any special problems relating to his past, and to tell the family doctor. Other parents tell everyone quite openly – one mother always introduced her daughter as 'my adopted daughter' from the beginning. This is really a matter of personal choice.

Some parents who adopt older children find that it is very helpful for them and the child to make up a 'life story book' of the child's own. This book contains all the details of the child's life, any information known about his natural parents, where he has lived, and so on. This is something which social workers are recognizing as increasingly valuable for older children who have lived in a number of foster homes or institutions, because it helps them to understand what has happened to them and gives their life a pattern, and this may well have been done over a prolonged period as part of the child's preparation for a move to a new family. Without understanding and coming to terms with the past, it may be very difficult to face the future. It also helps the child to fit his memories into the structure of events in his life.

Sometimes when a child comes to a family he will already have a life story book, but more often it will be up to the parents to compile it. This can involve writing to the foster families or institutions where the child has lived asking for dates, photographs, and any information that will help the child to remember. Letters from the house mother or foster mother can be kept in the book, together with any other mementoes. Often the child becomes very involved and interested in compiling the book and may like to add to it, draw in it, colour it and make it his own. Parents often find this a very valuable way of getting close to the child and letting him understand that they care about him, rather than deciding to conceal and forget about his past. Even if some memories are painful, it is better for the child to remember than to repress them, although obviously you wouldn't want to dwell on things he finds difficult or painful.

If you child is black or of mixed race, you can use such a book as an opportunity to explain the child's background. You can find maps or pictures of the child's country of origin, if appropriate, and write a little about it. However, the child is likely to have been born in Britain so it is important not to confuse him about his nationality.

Some parents find that the child seems to accept the adoption story well at one stage, and then appears to become distressed by it. Often this coincides with the child developing a new awareness of what is meant by it:

At the age of about ten Cathy suddenly started to ask all sorts of questions about her birth mother, who we always called by her name, Alison. She wanted to know where she had been born and who her father was and so on. Eventually, talking to another mother, I realised that the school had shown the class a film about how babies were born, culminating with a film of a birth. No wonder she had become so suddenly interested.

I rang up the school and spoke to her form teacher, explaining that the film had caused Cathy some confusion and complaining that we hadn't been warned. It didn't do any harm, and I wouldn't have wanted her not to see it, but it would have helped to have prepared her a little and to have been able to answer all her questions more appropriately.

Despite the most careful thought and preparation, some children are upset by knowing the truth about their past, especially if it has been a very unhappy or confusing one. Being rejected by a parent is a very hard fact to face and understand, and many adoptive parents know that, even though they try to take the natural parents' side and explain why they couldn't keep the child, nothing would induce them to part with the child, a fact which they too have to explain. Children may take out some of their pain and confusion on their new parents, especially in the early period after adoption:

I remember he would screw himself right up and say, 'You're not my real father!' when I told him he had to do something he didn't want. The first time you could have heard a pin drop in the silence after he'd spoken. But I said, 'I don't care if I'm your real father or not, I'm looking after you now and you're going to do what I say'. And bit by bit it lost its force.

Similarly, some adopted children use the fact that they have not always lived with their present family as a threat when things don't happen as they would like. Occasionally, especially in the early days, they might threaten to want to return to the nursery or to their foster home. This can be hard to cope with unless the adoptive family are secure enough not to pay it too much attention. After all, natural children sometimes threaten to leave home as well.

81

Because adopting a child can bring with it special problems, especially if the child is handicapped, is older and has behavioural problems, or is black or of mixed race, most adoptive parents want particularly to be able to rely on the support and help of family and close friends. Not all adoptive parents find their families understanding, especially in the beginning, although most in the end come to love and accept the child.

> We didn't get a lot of support from anyone – people thought we were crazy to take on a handicapped baby. They said we were tying ourselves up for the rest of our lives – everyone we mentioned it to said, 'But are you really wise to adopt her? What about when she's 20?' But now at least my mother thinks she's wonderful. Other people find their family less than understanding.

Friends and neighbours, being less emotionally involved than grandparents, may be more helpful and supportive. The older generation probably carry with them all kinds of prejudices about adoption which do not fit in with today's way of thinking, and feel that adopting a child is in some way shameful. Others, of course, will understand the reasons why the child has been adopted and welcome them with all their hearts.

Another emotional and difficult area in bringing up an adopted child is helping the child to trace his or her natural parents. Under the Children Act 1975 all adopted people over the age of eighteen have the right to have access to their original birth records. This information is not necessarily intended for the purpose of tracing parents, though this may be the hope in a minority of cases. Everyone adopted before the Act came into force must receive counselling from a social worker before the information is made available to them and people adopted since can have counselling if they wish. Some adoptive parents may know more about the natural parents and have had some contact with them, and consider putting the child in touch before this if they really want to, though this is very rare.

The birth certificate will only give the child's parents' names and place of residence at the time of the birth, so tracing them can be very difficult, especially if the mother has remarried and changed her name or moved away from the area in which she lived. Previous foster parents or staff in a children's home may have had contact with the natural parents and know something more recent of them. Sometimes natural parents who would like their children to get in touch can write a letter to the Registrar General in the hope that their child makes an application to see the birth certificate. There is also an organization called NORCAP which helps adopted people who are trying to contact their natural parents as well as parents who have given up their children. (See list of useful addresses.)

In fact, only a very small percentage of adopted people decide to trace their natural parents, and it is not an indication that they have been unhappy in their new families. Some children might have vague or even clear memories of their natural parents, others might want some gaps filled in. Sometimes it is some other factor which makes an adopted person want to get in touch:

It was when I had my own child and I realized that, whenever I gave a medical history, there were all kinds of things I didn't know. It also struck me with terrifying force when Jamie was born that he was the first person I had ever seen who was blood related to me. Even now I cannot get over how similar he is to me, not only in looks but personality.

This reawoke in me a desire to see what my own mother had been like, and to find some answers to some questions about my own and Jamie's health. In fact, it was not too difficult to trace her and I wrote to her asking if she would like to see me, explaining that I was happily married with a child and that one meeting would satisfy me. I said that I didn't want to interfere with her life in any way and would quite understand if she didn't want to see me.

We did meet, and I found to my surprise that she wasn't really like me at all. We didn't seem to have much in common, all our attitudes about life were different; she was the kind of person who accepted everything as fate and never tried to change her life, while I had accepted from my adopted parents that life is yours for the making. She had, however, looked out some old family photographs and documents for me which she said I could have as she had no use for them, and she did fill me in about her family's medical history. We parted amicably enough and I gave her my address, but she has never got in touch or showed any desire to see Jamie.

Adoptive parents may find the idea of a child contacting the natural parents threatening, but there is no reason why this should be so. The natural parents have no claim on them, and the child will be legally of age anyway, and free to make any kind of choice about their lives. In fact, talking it through with the child can bring some families closer, and if the child does, as happens in very rare instances, get involved in the life of the natural parent, this relationship can be a very positive one for them. Fears that the natural parent will in some way steal the child away are completely unfounded.

Some adopted people want to trace their natural parents because they know that they had brothers or sisters and want to get in touch with them. Again, such contact can be very rewarding, although often the siblings have little in common:

> I got in touch with my 'real' mother because I knew that I had a younger sister, and we arranged a meeting. When I saw my sister, it was a bit of a shock, because no one told me that she was only a half-sister or that her father, unlike mine, was black! We were completely different people, had led completely different lives, and it was plain that she really had no time for me. I felt very uncomfortable and I must say that it really blew all my fantasies about this darling little sister with blonde curly hair and pink ribbons!
>
> For that reason, I'm very glad I traced her, and I will send her news like if we move or I get married, just in case our paths cross again one day.

The bonds made by years of living together are likely to be far more important in the end than bonds of blood, although this adopted child, now grown up with a family of her own, feels that in the end neither count as much as friendship:

I realized in the end that it has more to do with personalities than blood links. I still adore my adoptive father, who, though he separated from my mother and went abroad, still writes me the most wonderful caring letters. My adoptive mother I always found more hard to understand, so I don't see so much of her, and in fact I probably see more of my blood mother, with whom I get on very well. I have an adoptive sister, who I grew up with, with whom I'm very close, and a 'real' half-sister, who I don't like at all. But as you get older you choose the people you want to be with, and it doesn't really matter who's related any more.

If adoption goes wrong

Very occasionally adoptions do not work out. No matter how difficult the problems, most families are prepared to see them through; the agency Parents for Children, which finds homes for very hard-to-place children, have had only one adoption break down in ten years, despite the severity of the children's handicaps or emotional problems. Very rarely, however, an adoption will break down after it has been legalized. In fact, there is no procedure by which you can 'divorce' a child. It is, in effect, as if things have gone wrong between you and a natural child. In the vast majority of cases it would only be possible to revoke an adoption in very unusual circumstances such as where there had been deception or a procedural irregularity. You may be able to come to some family arrangement, send a child to boarding school or to a special residential school, or arrange for the child to stay with family or friends. Or, with the help of the social worker, you may be able to arrange for the child to return to an institution or to a foster home, or even, in the end, to be placed for adoption again.

Support after adoption

Many parents do feel isolated when they face problems with their adopted children because they may not know other families who have adopted, with whom they can discuss their experiences.

Many adoption agencies now offer a post-adoption service, especially for those who have adopted children with special needs, but sometimes talking to other adoptive parents is all that is needed. Parent to parent information on adoption services (PPIAS) is one organization which provides invaluable support to adoptive parents by putting them in touch with other people locally who share their experiences:

> Whenever we had problems with Sophie we had felt terribly isolated till I heard about PPIAS. Through them I met other adoptive mothers and was relieved to find that they experienced similar emotions and fears as I did. I also discovered that many of these problems were shared by 'ordinary' families – but I didn't have the confidence to believe that until I'd been able to share my worries with other adoptive parents. They provided us with invaluable help in telling Sophie about her background and were also splendid when we decided to adopt a second, handicapped baby – they gave us so much support and I made friends without whom I don't think we could have considered such a move, as we relied on them a lot!

A list of helpful organizations is provided in the appendix.

6

Fostering

Many people who find themselves unable to adopt, perhaps because they are too old or because they feel unable to take on children with handicaps or behavioural problems, consider fostering as an alternative. However, adoption and fostering are very different, and fostering should not be considered as a 'back door' to adoption by those parents who have not been accepted by adoption agencies. Foster parents have to accept that the child or children in their care are going to be with them only for a time, either till they return to their natural families or until an adoptive home is found for them. Foster parents will have to remain in close touch with the social services and important decisions about the future of the child will be made by them, perhaps with help from the foster family. A foster parent also often has to keep the relationship between children and their natural parents alive if the plan is that they should be returned to them.

Some fostering is very short-term, and is used to help families in times of crisis. For instance, if a mother has to go into hospital to have another baby and there is no-one to care for her other children, or during a divorce or severe illness in the family, the children may go to a foster home for a few weeks till they can return home, rather than going to an institution. Here the foster parents are really acting as friends of the family would, by taking in their children till the crisis is over. Occasionally the situation is less clear-cut; the child's family may have had problems for some time and the child been disturbed or perhaps neglected. Social workers will however be trying to help sort out the family's problems and the foster parents will need to care for the child in the meantime and help him look forward to returning home.

Sometimes children might stay with foster families for some months. A foster placement which lasts for more than six months is usually referred to as long stay, and many children remain with foster families for a considerable period. Quite often the time that the child is likely to stay for is not clear at the outset. The aim is to provide care for the child till a decision is reached about his future, and this can take some time, till it is clear whether the child can ever return to his family. Long-stay fostering therefore requires considerable skills and selflessness on the part of the foster parents, who have to build a close relationship with the child, care for him as if he were their own, and yet be prepared for him to leave for another family. Foster parents are often involved with prospective adopters when they come to visit the child, and this can be the cause of much tension if the foster parents would really like to adopt the child themselves. They may feel that they are much more suitable than the adopting couple, or that they are being passed over for reasons they do not understand.

Permanent fostering also exists to cater for those children who can never return to their natural families and who, for some reason, cannot be adopted. The natural parents may for example refuse to allow the child to be adopted and the adoption agency be uncertain that an adoption order would be granted against the parents' wishes if it went to court. Here fostering is very similar to adoption and, in fact, the Children Act 1975 allows for a new kind of arrangement called custodianship which will be half-way between adoption and fostering to apply to such situations. Custodianship orders will be made by the court and will last until the child reaches the age of eighteen unless revoked by the court at the request of either the natural parents or custodians. While the order is in force, custodians carry out almost all the normal parental responsibilities including all the day-to-day decisions in a child's life, but they are not able to change the child's name or break all contact with the natural parents.

The idea is that foster parents and children who have been together for a long period will have more security, so that the child cannot be removed at short notice and important decisions, for example about education, cannot be made over the foster parents' heads. For similar reasons, since 1976, foster parents who have cared for a child for five years or more have an automatic right to an adoption hearing if they want one. The foster parents have to notify the local authority that they are applying for an adoption order, and the children then cannot be removed from them until the application is heard in court. This does not of course mean that the adoption will be always granted, but it does mean that the foster parents have a chance to put their case if they would like to adopt. It also recognizes the fact that after such a period of time the child is likely to have become very attached to his foster family and even regard them as his proper parents, and that it is likely to be in his best interests to live with them permanently without the fear of being removed, to take their name, and so on.

Some foster parents specialize in taking on particular kinds of children, especially if they are taking them only for the short term. For instance, a foster mother might take in small babies until they are found adoptive parents; this obviously requires special skills in looking after small babies, and someone who enjoys caring for them may find it very rewarding to give them a good start in life and hand them on to their new families. Others might take in teenagers, others children with particular handicaps with which they are familiar. Some foster parents become real professionals at their jobs, taking in many children over their fostering careers and finding tremendous fulfilment from it.

Foster parents do not have to be married couples with experience of looking after children, although this may help. Single people, older couples, single parents and even people with handicaps may all make excellent foster parents. If you are interested in applying to be a foster parent, you need to contact your local authority and ask for the fostering officer within the social services department. Most local authorities are looking for more foster parents and are likely to welcome your enquiry. They will probably arrange for a social worker to visit you to discuss foster care, the kinds of children they need to find homes for and whether you would be able to help.

Potential foster parents are assessed just as would-be adopters are assessed, to make sure that they understand their role and responsibilities and can be entrusted with the care of a child. Your background will be looked into and sometimes foster parents are expected to attend special training courses: if they are going to look after black or mixed-race children, for example, they might be expected to attend a course on racism awareness. Some special foster schemes exist to help children with particular problems, such as disturbed or delinquent teenagers or children with particular handicaps, and the foster parents may be paid on a higher level than traditional foster parents though technically they are not staff and do not receive a salary. Almost invariably foster parents involved in such schemes will have special training.

Most foster parents receive allowances to cover the cost of looking after their foster child or children. The amount depends on the local authority and the age of the child and any special needs which they have, but it is far from generous, and no-one would really consider fostering as a way of earning a living. There are other allowances which you might be able to claim if you are looking after a handicapped child such as the mobility allowance or attendance allowance, and the local authority should be able to help you in applying for these. (See also section on handicapped children in Chapter 3).

Children living in a foster home for any length of time do face some considerable difficulties in adjusting to their situation, because it is an ambiguous one. Many foster parents and professionals consider foster care as second best to adoption, though few would deny that foster homes are better than institutional care for most children. The child may be uncertain, as are those around him, as to whether and when he is likely to go back to his family, and he may be hurt and confused as to why he has come into care. Not knowing is very hard for a child to deal with, as he can neither put his past behind him and get on with adjusting to a new family nor look forward confidently into the future. How can he develop plans and goals for the future when he doesn't know what it will hold, or even know where he will be next Christmas? Many foster parents say that they are inhibited by not being able to talk about 'What we'll do when you're older' or 'Where we'll go next year'. The child may also be uncertain whether to call his foster parents Mum and Dad or whether to reserve that for his natural parents with whom he may or may not be reunited.

Some foster parents feel frustrated by the fact that they cannot make decisions on behalf of the child and feel that this puts him or her in an insecure position:

> We want to adopt her for her own security. We could get a new social worker who said, 'I don't think you're the right family for this child – I'm going to move her', and they could move her without a day's noice. If she got to eighteen they could decide to put her in a home for mentally handicapped adults or whatever they liked, while we have all kinds of plans which I'm sure would be better for her.

Others find that they are coping with the results of poor decisions made by the social services:

> We had been fostering the boys for about eighteen months when they decided they were going back to their natural mother. She came to see them a few times and I must say, I didn't trust her an inch, and I even said to the social worker look, this isn't going to work. But they knew best, so I had to prepare the boys and they were both very excited that they were going back and I think also sad to be leaving us. But I presented it all in a very positive light and on the day they packed up, there weren't too many tears. Well, off they went, and three months later they were back, I can't tell you how changed. Their mother had got a new boyfriend and he had knocked them around. They looked as if they hadn't had a square meal in the entire time they were away and they were upset, bewildered and withdrawn. I think they felt we had betrayed them somehow in telling them how good it was going to be. We were back to wet sheets, tantrums, stealing, truanting – all the problems we had so carefully helped them over in the time they'd been with us.
>
> Now the mother is saying she wants them back again, she's ditched the boyfriend, everything is hunkydory. I would say to the social worker, I won't have her in the house, but I'm afraid if I did that they'd put them somewhere else, and I feel we're the only security they've got.

Many long-term foster parents would, in fact, prefer adoption if it were possible. It seems obvious that after a while the child will form links with them rather than with the natural parents, ask to call them Mummy and Daddy, make friends in the neighbourhood and feel they belong there; the foster parents too feel that the child is 'theirs'. 'It's only human nature, you can't deny it,' said one foster mother. 'You can try not to get too fond of them, but in the end you just can't stop yourself.'

Foster placements disrupt much more readily than adoptive ones; in some areas of the country as many as fifty per cent break down while adoption breakdowns are very rare. This is probably because being a foster parent is by nature and intention temporary, so they cannot feel the same commitment to the children as those who have a permanent arrangement; they also may not feel they are in control. The foster parent has to try to retain some emotional distance from the child, and this does not help when things go badly: 'If he was my child I'd put up with it. But he's got to go sooner or later, so I suppose I thought, it might as well be sooner, all the trouble he's causing.' Another reason is undoubtedly lack of adequate support from the social services – in special schemes where foster parents are given training and a lot of back-up support the rate of breakdown is much lower.

Sometimes, too, the presence of natural parents creates intolerable tensions for foster parents and children. The children may feel a tug of loyalty between the two sets of parents and may find it disturbing to be reminded of their natural parents inadequacy and rejection, which makes them more unsettled and disturbed. Some foster parents find themselves trying to help the natural parents against their will:

> She used to come round to visit her son and sit there pouring out all her woes to me. She was only about nineteen – I suppose she looked on me as a kind of substitute mother. But I really didn't feel it was my job to counsel her, and it used to annoy me, because she'd come when she pleased and often put my whole day out. She also never took any notice of Stephen; I'd ask her what she thought about this or that that he was doing and she'd just say 'Oh', or 'I don't know.'

Other foster parents do manage to build a good and constructive relationship with the natural parents, successfully building a bridge between them and the child in preparation for their return. Sometimes foster parents continue to help the child relate to their natural parents even though there seems no hope of their ever getting reunited:

> Michelle's mother had been in a mental hospital two or three times, never had any money, a job or a stable home, and had a series of relationships with immature and exploitative men. It soon became obvious that she would never be able to give Michelle a proper home, but she was her mother, was fond of the child in her way, and came to visit her often, every week or two. Michelle used to look forward to her visits though she didn't always enjoy them so much while they were happening, but I would always ring up and check and remind her that she was coming and what time so Michelle wouldn't be disappointed. I had to explain over and over why Michelle couldn't live with her mother and make excuses when she let her down again.

This attitude – considered by the professionals as the 'correct' one – may end up by doing more harm to the child by confronting him with a parent who for some reason, probably inexplicable to the child, does not want to care for him. These children may find their relationship with the foster parents is affected and feel that they do not know where they belong.

Fostering children can clearly be a very rewarding job for many people and give them a chance to share in the problems and joys of parenthood. However, long-term fostering is clearly a very difficult role for the parents to play, as many must be forced to put aside their natural feelings of condemnation for parents who show almost limitless irresponsibility towards their children. For this reason it is probably much better that people who would really like to adopt do not put themselves in such a painful position, with the risk of the placement disrupting and the child being further disturbed, as caring for a child in the long term who they can never call their own.

Useful Addresses

Be My Parent
c/o *BAAF* (address below)
Tel: 01–407 9763

Book produced by BAAF containing two hundred photographs and descriptions of children with special needs looking for families. Telephone for information on where the nearest book can be seen.

British Agencies for Adoption and Fostering (BAAF)
11 Southwark Street
London SE1 1RQ
Tel: 01–407 8800

Promotes good standards of practice in adoption and fostering and aims to increase public understanding of the social, legal, medical and psychological issues involved in adoption. BAAF provides an advisory service and publishes the booklet 'Adopting a Child' each year giving up-to-date information for would-be adopters.

Contact a Family
16 Strutton Ground
London SW1P 2HP
Tel: 01–222 2695

Brings together families of physically and mentally handicapped children within the same neighbourhood to form self-help family groups.

Down's Children's Association
3rd Floor, Horne's Premises, 4 Oxford Street
London W1N 9FL
Tel: 01–580 0511/2

A self-help group which has branches and groups throughout the country to provide support for parents of Down's Syndrome children. It also promotes research into the causes and effects of Down's Syndrome.

Family Rights Group
6 Manor Gardens
Holloway Road
London N7 6LA
Tel: 01–272 4231/7308

Works for the rights of parents when their children are taken into care.

Harmony
22 St Mary's Road
Meare
Glastonbury
Somerset BA6 9SP
Tel: (04586) 311

An association for racially mixed families which helps parents to bring up black and mixed-race children to feel positive about their identities.

MENCAP
The Royal Society for Mentally Handicapped Children and Adults
123 Golden Lane
London EC1Y 0RT
Tel: 01–253 9433

Offers support for mentally handicapped people and their families through its network of 450 local societies.

National Association for the Childless (NAC)
318 Summer Lane
Birmingham
B19 3RL
Tel: (021) 359 4887

Counsels people with infertility problems, supports the childless and helps them to find a fulfilled lifestyle, and assists with overseas adoption.

National Foster Care Association
Francis House
Francis Street
London SW1P 1DE
Tel: 01–828 6266/7

Encourages a high standard of foster care and seeks better opportunities for children in care to find foster homes.

National Organisation for Counselling Adoptees and their Parents (NORCAP)
10 Piers Close
Warwick
CU34 5HS
Tel: (0926) 498 535

Provides support to adult adopted people and both their adoptive and birth parents. Helps adult adopted people who are trying to get in touch with their birth parents and has a register of both adoptees and birth relatives seeking to make contact.

Parents for Children
222 Camden High Street
London NW1 8QR
Tel: 01–485 7526/48

An agency which finds parents for hard-to-place children in the London area.

Parent to Parent Information on Adoptive Services (PPIAS)
Lower Boddington
Daventry
Northamptonshire NN11 6YB
Tel: (0327) 60295

Helps potential adopters by passing on information about how and where to apply for children, especially those with special needs, and also from overseas. Local groups also give support to members who have adopted or are in the process of doing so.

Further Reading

Austin, Judy, ed. *Adoption The Inside Story*. Barn Owl Books 1985
Available from *Parent to Parent Information on Adoption Services*

Tizard, Barbara, *Adoption: A Second Chance*. Open Books 1977

Macaskill, Catherine, *Against the Odds, Adopting Mentally Handicapped Children*. British Agencies for Adoption and Fostering 1985

Argent, Hedi, *Find me a Family – The story of* Parents for Children. Souvenir Press 1984

Cunningham, Cliff, and Sloper, Patricia, *Helping your Handicapped Baby*. Souvenir Press 1978

Rowe, Jane, *Yours by Choice – A Guide for Adoptive Parents*. Routledge and Kegan Paul, new edition 1982

Rowe, Jane, and Lambert, Lydia, *Children who Wait*. Association of British Adoption Agencies 1973

Gill, Owen, and Jackson, Barbara, *Adoption and Race – Black, Asian and Mixed-race Children in White Families*. (Batsford 1983)